Turning
Wealth
into
What
Matters

A LDE
Spark Generosity for Mission

Kurtis Smith
Bethany Global Univ

For Lowla and Charlie

DANA HOLT
JD, RICP, AEP® CAP®

Turning Wealth into What Matters

A Practical Step-by-Step Guide
to Accepting Non-Cash Gifts

Paperback ISBN: 9781952976346
LCCN: 2022900773

Cover Design: Casey Fuerst

Interior Design: Ann Aubitz

First Printing: April 2022

First Edition

Published by Kirk House Publishers
1250 E 115th Street
Burnsville, MN 55337
Kirkhousepublishers.com
612-781-2815

Table of Contents

How To Use This Book

This book is designed as a practical, step-by-step guide to help you establish or expand your non-cash gift capabilities. It focuses on the most common situations you will encounter when dealing with non-cash gifts. It does not cover every possible situation.

Chapter 1 will help you wrap your head around the world of non-cash gifts, donor motivations, working with advisors, and to set yourself up for success.

Chapters 2-9 address specific assets. Each chapter starts off with practical advice, including a 5-step process you can use to investigate, evaluate, accept, or decline a gift of a non-cash asset. At the end of each chapter, you'll find *sample* Procedures, Asset Questionnaires, Gift Instructions, and in some cases Deeds of Gift. These documents are meant as samples to help you get started. They should each be adapted to your organization's specific needs. I highly encourage you to consult with your legal and tax counsel to make sure that the documents you use are appropriate for your organization and in your state.

Do NOT skip right to the sample documents and overlook the practical advice section of the chapter. You will miss essential detail vital to the success or failure of a gift.

Chapter 10 takes a close look at Donor Advised Funds because they play a gigantic role in the world of non-cash gifts. It is very important you know how they work and how to use them to your advantage.

Chapter 11 summarizes some of the most important points of the book and gives advice for continuing your expertise when it comes to non-cash gift planning.

When performing detailed due diligence on a proposed non-cash gift, I encourage you to consult additional resources for a detailed explanation of legal and tax rules, including your legal counsel. I can recommend wonderful options. First, *Charitable Gifts of Noncash Assets* by Bryan Clontz. You can order a hard copy or download a free PDF online. Second, *GiftLaw Pro* from Crescendo Interactive. It is also free to view on their website. Neither HOLT Consulting, LLC, nor Dana Holt are affiliated with these companies and neither receives any compensation for these recommendations.

Charitable giving can result in significant tax, legal, and financial consequences. Neither HOLT Consulting, LLC, nor Dana J. Holt provides legal, accounting, or tax advice. You should consult your legal and tax advisors to determine how each individual gift situation will affect your donors and your organization.

To ensure compliance with IRS requirements, be aware that any U.S. federal tax advice that may be contained in this book is not intended or written to be used, and cannot be used, for the purpose of (i) avoiding penalties under the Internal Revenue Code or (ii) promoting, marketing and recommending to another party any transaction or matter addressed herein.

Chapter 1: Get Ready for Non-Cash Gifts

At some point in your fundraising career, a donor will ask if she can donate a non-cash gift, like a home or virtual currency. Non-cash gifts can feel daunting and sometimes even scary. You'll be concerned whether you have the time and expertise necessary to evaluate and manage the asset. What if it becomes more work than you can handle? What if you can't sell it? What if it subjects your organization to significant risk? Not to worry, this book will help you uncover the opportunity that non-cash gifts can bring to your organization and enable you to have confident conversations with donors about non-cash gifts.

This book will help to eliminate the fears you have when it comes to non-cash gifts. It will provide you with:

- Fundamental knowledge for each type of asset,
- A step-by-step process you can use to evaluate and accept virtually any non-cash gift,
- Proven internal procedures you can begin using right away, and
- Detailed intake checklists so you can be sure to collect all the right information about the asset from the donor.

The next time someone offers a non-cash gift, you will be able to *confidently* answer YES or NO, and *WHY*.

THE NUMBERS...

If you've picked up this book, you've probably read some of the research on non-cash gifts.

1. Non-cash assets make up more than 90% of American wealth.[1]
2. Yet, more than 85% of the dollars given to charity every year are still in the form of cash.[2]
3. Charities that accept non-cash gifts raise up to 66% more money than those that don't.[3]

We know that non-cash gifts offer an outstanding opportunity for nonprofits, but only a small fraction of charities are accepting them. ***Our fears are keeping us from seizing the opportunity.***

Before we dive into learning about asset types and procedures for evaluating and accepting non-cash gifts, we need to set the stage a bit. In this chapter, we will:
1. **Learn *WHEN* non-cash gifts happen,**
2. **Get to know your donor's financial situation,**
3. **Outline the best way to design a non-cash gift plan,**
4. **Explore the important role professional advisors play in charitable planning, and**
5. **Outline *HOW* to build your non-cash giving program.**

WHEN DO NON-CASH GIFTS HAPPEN?

Very few people wake up one morning and say to themselves,

"Hey, I want to donate a non-cash asset to my favorite charity!"

They probably think from time to time about how nice it would be to make a significant charitable gift, but something else is usually the catalyst that makes it happen. That *something else* is what I call a **life event.**

---

[1] James, Russell, PhD. *"Cash is Not King in Fundraising: Gifts of Non-Cash Assets Predicts Contributions Growth"* (2018)
[2] Aggregate IRS tax return data (2012)
[3] James, Russell, PhD. *"Cash is Not King in Fundraising: Gifts of Non-Cash Assets Predicts Contributions Growth"* (2018)

When talking with a donor, it's essential to listen for signs of these life events. These are times when donors will be motivated to put their biggest charitable goals into action:

Event	Possible Gift Type
Finish college/graduate school and begin career.	Name charity as beneficiary of retirement account or life insurance policy.
Welcome first child to the family.	- Create first Will/Trust. - Update beneficiary designations on retirement accounts and life insurance. - Include charity as beneficiary of Will/Trust and/or financial accounts.
Exercise stock options at work or rebalance stock portfolio. Both create extra taxable income.	Shares of stock available to give to charity and income tax deduction helpful to offset extra income.
Children graduate from college.	No more tuition payments. Assets freed up for increased charitable giving.
Welcome first grandchild to the family.	Update Will/Trust to include grandchild. Update/include charitable beneficiaries.
Retirement.	Assess how much wealth is needed in retirement and which assets are no longer needed/wanted. Assets freed up to donate to charity.
Sale of business, creating a large influx of taxable income.	Consider donating some of the business stock to charity before sale. Alternatively, may donate cash to charity after the sale.
Spouse passes away	- Update Will/Trust and Beneficiary Designations to include charities. - Potential downsizing of residence and donation of real estate. - Assets freed up for increased charitable giving.

UNDERSTANDING YOUR DONOR'S FINANCIAL SITUATION

Many donors who contemplate making a significant non-cash gift during life are probably retired or close to retirement. They know they have more assets than they will need for retirement and probably more than they want to leave to heirs. They feel confident that they can live a comfortable retirement and still have wealth to share.

Retirees no longer have paychecks from work. A gift from cash flow is probably the most financially painful gift they could make and probably the most tax-*inefficient*. Their retirement cash flow is designed to cover things like daily expenses, bills, and vacations. That cash flow comes mostly from Social Security, pensions, and distributions from retirement accounts. All of those income types are taxed at their highest income tax rates, so they're going to try to keep that kind of income as low as possible. There isn't going to be much cash left over for charitable giving.

Furthermore, at the time of writing, interest rates are at historically low levels and have been there for a long time. If someone has financial wealth they're not using, it doesn't make sense to keep it in a cash account that pays almost no interest. A wealth advisor would recommend keeping enough cash to cover large upcoming expenses and emergencies, but to invest the rest in something else that pays a larger return. That may be stocks or rental real estate or other non-cash assets. Cash flow and cash reserves are managed carefully and not designed to produce a lot of excess. This is why we *must* look beyond cash flow and cash reserves for charitable gifts.

DESIGNING THE BEST NON-CASH GIFT PLAN

Once you've determined that a donor is ready to make a significant gift, you'll need to know how to develop a gift plan. Gift Plans should be created in 3 steps and those steps must be taken in a specific order. *Get them out of order and the plan is very likely to crumble.*
1. **Goals**
2. **Tools**
3. **Techniques**

GIFT PLAN STEP 1: GOALS

Developing charitable goals is not something most people spend a lot of time doing. You're probably very good at helping people uncover their charitable desires. Otherwise, you probably wouldn't be working in gift planning.

Goal Development is the MOST IMPORTANT step in the 3-step Gift Plan process. Unless you fully <u>understand what you're trying to accomplish</u>, it's impossible to achieve a successful result. You'll probably spend 75% or more of your time on goal development, and that's a good thing.

Here are some of my favorite questions to ask to get the goal development ball rolling. I call them "Conversation Sparklers". You may already be using these same questions.
- What is your earliest memory of giving?
- Is there someone you admire who shaped who you are?
- Who is the most generous person you know and why?
- How did/do your parents/grandparents practice generosity? Does that influence the way you give?

It's helpful to think about developing a charitable goal the same way you'd develop another kind of goal. Let's say you want to build a new home. You hire an architect to design your new home. She will need to know some basic information first. How many people will live in the home? Will it be a full-time residence or vacation home? Do you like to cook and/or entertain? Can you navigate stairs, or will you need a single level? Based on your answers to questions like these, she can design a home and tell you how much it will cost.

Charitable giving goals should be approached in a similar manner. What problem are you trying to solve? What difference do you want to see in the world? How many meals do you want to provide per year to hungry children? How many students do you want to send to college?

Once someone thinks about the changes they want to make and can articulate them, you can tell them how much it will cost. It's very possible that the cost will be greater than their extra cash-flow or cash reserves. **That's when conversations about non-cash gifts begin - and that brings us to *Step 2 - Tools*.**

GIFT PLAN STEP 2: TOOLS

Assets are tools that help us achieve our goals. The assets a donor has in her toolbox will allow her to achieve her charitable goals. Not all assets are created equally. Some are better to give during life and some are better to give after death. We will get into those details in later chapters, but for now, here are some of the more common assets that people will give during life:
- Publicly Traded Stock/Mutual Funds
- Qualified Charitable Distribution from IRAs
- Real Estate
- Farmland

- Virtual Currency
- Harvested Crops
- Farm Machinery
- Life Insurance Policy

Determining the right asset to give requires the advice of financial and/or tax professionals. Don't try to figure this one out on your own. Bring in the donor's advisors to help with this step. Some donors don't have experienced advisors. That's why it's good for your organization to cultivate what I call your *"bench"*. You need a group of financial, legal, and tax advisors you trust who can give you and/or your donors the very best advice.

You should probably have at least three of each of the following on your "bench" to recommend to donors:
- **Certified Financial Planners**
- **Certified Public Accountants**
- **Estate Planning Attorneys**

Let the donors interview the advisors you recommend and choose those they like best. Make sure these advisors are passionate about charitable gift planning and have the best credentials.

What kinds of credentials should you look for?

Financial Advisors

There are a LOT of people who work in the financial services industry. Some sell products. Others sell advice. Some sell both. When it comes to charitable planning, I'm a big fan of advisors who specialize in giving quality advice. You may want to seek out those who hold a *Certified Financial Planner* designation (CFP®). They tend to sell advice and sometimes also products. To earn that designation, they complete a comprehensive and rigorous training process in a wide range of disciplines. They are required to receive continuing education and are held to a *"fiduciary standard"* when working with clients. That means they are legally bound to always do what is in the best interest of their clients—regardless of how it affects them. This is important in the world of gift planning.

Here's an example to illustrate this point. A donor may be best served donating stock that her wealth advisor manages. Wealth advisors are often paid based on a percentage of the assets they manage. If assets are removed from that portfolio and donated to charity, it could reduce the advisor's compensation. Someone held to a *fiduciary standard* must advise the client based on the *client's* best interest—not their own—or face serious penalties.

Tax Advisors

When it comes to Certified Public Accountants (CPAs), some work as "tax preparers" and some work as "tax planners". You're going to want to work with those who help clients with *tax planning*.

Tax preparers typically help clients file their tax returns for the previous year. Tax planners help clients plan for taxes in future years. They tend to charge more, but good advice never comes cheap and often saves more money in the long run.

Attorneys

There are as many types of attorneys as there are fish in the sea. Everyone has a specialty these days. Rarely do you find an attorney who doesn't specialize. The law is complex and gets more complex every year. This has forced attorneys to specialize—just like physicians. In the case of charitable gift planning, you'll want an attorney who specializes in the areas of estate, tax, and charitable planning. Many larger law firms actually have estate and charitable departments.

Your "bench" can also serve as advisors for your organization. You should be able to go to them for advice as well. They may also be good people to serve on your board. Their expertise can be of great value when planning for your organization's future.

When interviewing advisors to serve on the "bench" be sure to ask them for stories of clients they've helped with charitable planning, and also ask them whether they enjoy volunteering. You'll want people who are personally interested in charitable work.

A growing number of professional advisors (wealth advisors, accountants, and attorneys) and fundraisers have begun to pursue the *Chartered Advisor in Philanthropy* (CAP®) designation. In my experience, those who pursue this credential have a particular passion for charitable planning.

Advisors will help your donor to develop financial, tax, and estate plans that achieve both their philanthropic and financial goals. Through that process, they will identify the best assets to donate to achieve those goals.

Once the donor has identified which assets are no longer needed for their own uses and available for giving, it's time to move onto *Step 3: Techniques*.

GIFT PLAN STEP 3: TECHNIQUES

The final step in any gift plan is to develop the giving *technique*. **The *technique* is the method for making the gift.**

Will the gift be made during life or after death? Will it be made directly to the charity or through a Donor Advised Fund? Will it involve a Charitable Remainder Trust or Charitable Gift Annuity? These are all *techniques*. If Steps 1 and 2 were done properly, choosing the right technique will be very easy.

For example, if a donor wants to make a significant gift, is over 70 ½ years of age, and tells you she has way too much taxable income from her IRA, a Qualified Charitable Distribution could be the best way for her to make a gift.

If the donor's goals are to make a gift and receive an income stream, then a CRT or CGA are probably good techniques to explore.

If the donor wants to contribute one large asset to benefit multiple charities, a Donor Advised Fund is a good technique to consider.

By the same token, if a donor hasn't expressed a desire for additional income, don't suggest a CRT or CGA. This may seem like a no-brainer, but I've encountered dozens of advisors and fundraisers who are so eager to impress the donor with their technical knowledge that they forget about the donor's goals and immediately jump to the most complex giving technique they can imagine. Stick to the donor's goals. It will make the process so much easier for everyone.

You know the opportunity that non-cash gifts can bring. You know the role that professional advisors play in charitable planning. You have a three-step process for every single gift you encounter.

Now, it's time to turn our attention to your specific organization. Let's look at how to build your organization's non-cash giving program.

BUILD YOUR NON-CASH GIVING PROGRAM

Before you can start asking donors to consider gifts of non-cash assets, you'll need to get prepared. You'll need to build some infrastructure so that you are well-positioned to accept non-cash gifts efficiently and effectively.

Over the years, I've identified the following *essential* steps to building a successful non-cash gift program:

1. Commit to Growth
2. Document Numerical Goals
3. Identify Your Needs
4. Seek Opportunities
5. Adjust Goals

1. Commit to Growth

It sounds really easy, but committing to growth can be complex and a bit unnerving. Committing to growth means committing to soliciting and accepting non-cash gifts and *everyone* must be on board: you, the board, and management.

Conversations around non-cash gifts can be tricky and bring out some people's fears of what they don't know. Some people in your organization may push back with these objections:

"Non-cash gifts take too long."
"We're not capable of doing that."
"It's too complex for us."

Here's how you can respond to those objections.

First, non-cash gifts do take a while to develop, but they are ten to twenty times as large as someone's average cash gift. The extra time is worth the investment. A little patience goes a *long way*. This book is going to show you the most efficient ways of accepting each type of non-cash gift so that you can cut down the time it takes to receive these valuable gifts.

Second, you may or may not be capable of accepting every non-cash gift, but closing yourself off to all of them is just giving into fear. This book will outline some of the basic things you'll need to know to decide which non-cash gifts you're prepared to accept on your own and which ones you'll need help with.

Thirdly, non-cash gifts do come with complexity, but with a little basic knowledge and some step-by-step procedures, that complexity will be greatly reduced. This book will give you both knowledge and efficiency.

2. Document Your Goals

I've said it before, and I'll say it again: you'll never know if you've succeeded if you don't know what you're trying to accomplish. You've got to develop your goals. Once you've done that, you can determine what you're going to need to get there and outline your plan for doing so.

I recommend developing short-term, mid-term, and long-term goals. What do you want your organization to look like in 1 year, 5 years, 10 years? It helps to break down these big goals into increments that are achievable over time. It's also great to be able to celebrate achieving your short-term goals so you don't have to wait 10 years to acknowledge your achievements.

3. Identify Your Needs

To achieve your goals, you're going to need some things to support you along the way. Here are some areas of need that every organization should cover before they can build a successful non-cash gift program.

- Financial
- Gift Acceptance Policies
- Staff
- Communications

Financial Needs

Travel

If someone wants to donate something like real estate, you'll need to go view the property. You'll probably need to travel to meet with donors and their advisors to discuss the gifts in detail. Virtual meetings are efficient, but don't always cut the mustard. When we're talking about gifts worth many thousands or even millions of dollars, nothing beats a face-to-face encounter.

Materials

You'll need to communicate to donors about the benefits of non-cash gifts. You may create these in-house. You may hire a designer/writer, or you may contract with a vendor to brand some of their ready-made materials. Either way, it's going to cost some money.

Technology

You'll need to illustrate gifts to donors and to track gifts properly. If you don't already have software to illustrate things like charitable gift annuities and charitable remainder trusts, you're going to want to get some. Many donors will need to balance their need for income with their desire to make a significant gift. They often do that by creating a gift that provides them with some income.

Additionally, you may need to invest in some new accounting software and/or a new donor data management system. Not all of them are capable of tracking non-cash gift data, so make sure you get one that is.

Your website is an essential piece of technology that requires regular maintenance. It's a living, breathing representation of your organization and often the first place where people learn about your mission. The website is no place to cut corners or pinch pennies. Good websites are really simple. They aren't a dumping ground for mountains of text. They tell the reader *exactly* what you do in simple terms. They also tell the reader *exactly* how they can support that mission through giving and volunteering.

Vendors

You'll probably need to rely on outside vendors for help with some of your work with non-cash gifts—at least in the beginning. It's smart to rely on the infrastructure of others, rather than trying to recreate the wheel yourself. Whether it's help with materials, financial tracking, or legal counsel, you'll want to allocate some budget to these helpers.

Gift Acceptance Policies

Gift Acceptance Policies have got to be the most boring topic of all when it comes to gift planning. They may be boring, but they are also ESSENTIAL to your success. You need to know which assets you will accept on your own and which ones you will farm out to a helper such as a community foundation. You'll need to know your minimums for each gift type as well. Well-written gift acceptance policies can help you get out of some sticky situations. If someone wants to donate something inappropriate or that just isn't worth the time and effort it would take to process it, you can cite your policies as the reason for declining the gift.

Do you have gift acceptance policies? If not, I advise looking for some free templates online to get you started. Many services, including the National Association of Charitable Gift Planners, have made these templates available for free. They should not be relied on word for word. You need to customize them to your organization's needs, but it's a heck of a lot easier than starting from scratch.

If you do have policies, when was the last time they were updated? Your policies should be put on a regular review schedule. I advise a complete review by the board and management no less than every three years. The world changes quickly and your policies need to be current and up to date. For example, if your policies haven't been reviewed for several years, they probably don't address virtual currency. Gift minimums can get out of date quickly too.

Make sure that you can always locate your policies, that they're current, and that you know whose responsibility it is to manage them.

As you develop and review your policies, I recommend consulting with an attorney who is experienced in advising nonprofits about these policies. A few hours of good legal advice can save you a TON of headaches down the road.

Staff

Staff is necessary to solicit and process non-cash gifts. You'll probably need gift officers to develop relationships with donors. You may need a gift administrator to keep track of vital data about donors and their gifts. You'll definitely need financial management staff to help evaluate potential non-cash gifts and to appropriately handle/liquidate the gifts once they've been accepted.

Staff is probably the most expensive area of need you'll have. It is essential that you employ staff who can have confident conversations with donors and their advisors. They also need to be able to spot opportunities for non-cash gifts. This book will go a long way to helping them get up to speed, but nothing compares to actual practice during on-the-job experience. So do your best to hire staff with non-cash gift experience. If that's not possible, invest in some quality professional development on non-cash gifts. There are some high-quality, affordable options out there.

Communications

You'll need a clear, concise communications plan each year. Think of all the different audiences you need to reach to spread the word about non-cash gifts. Make sure you don't leave any of them out. You don't need a completely different message for each group, but you should communicate in a way that shows you understand their relationship with your organization.

- Donors
- Prospects
- Professional Advisors
- Your Board of Directors
- The General Public
- Volunteers

If you don't have the resources to process all kinds of non-cash gifts, start with some easy-to-process but valuable gifts. Let everyone know you accept stock, mutual funds, grants from Donor Advised Funds, and Qualified Charitable Distributions from IRAs. Once these types of gifts start rolling in, they will provide you with extra resources to tackle the more complicated non-cash gifts.

Raising awareness is VITAL. People don't automatically think beyond their checkbooks when considering a charitable gift. Make it easy for them by communicating these options in multiple places and telling them EXACTLY where to go for instructions on how to do it. You may also consider outlining *brief* financial benefits of each one, but don't lead with that. Lead with your *mission* and stories of donors giving non-cash gifts.

Think of all the places you reach donors and be sure to mention your ability to accept these kinds of gifts. Let's take a look at some of the ways you communicate with your donors and how you can raise awareness of non-cash gifts.

Annual Appeals: When you send written appeals to donors, you probably list giving options such as "check" and "credit card". Consider adding a few more options:
- ***Gift of Stock or Mutual Funds*** (Be sure to tell readers exactly where they can get instructions on how to do so.)
- ***Request a Grant from my Donor Advised Fund***
- ***Qualified Charitable Distribution from my IRA***

Be sure to include your organization's:
- Official Name
- Address
- Federal Tax ID Number

Personal Visits: When talking to donors one-on-one, be sure to let them know that they can make gifts of stock or mutual funds, a grant from their Donor Advised Fund, or a QCD from their IRA. You may even want to develop a few simple pieces to leave with them that explain the benefits of these gift types. Don't get too technical. The best thing to include is a story of a donor who has done it, why they did it, and how it made them feel.

Your Website: It's a very good idea to create a simple page on your website that outlines the different assets you accept, simple financial benefits of that kind of gift, as well as a clear call to action for those who are interested in donating non-cash gifts.

4. Seek Opportunities

Opportunities for non-cash gifts are all around you. Before long, you'll begin to spot them at every turn.

Conversations with just about anyone are opportunities to plant seeds about non-cash gifts. Gather a few stories of donors making non-cash gifts. Be ready to tell those stories whenever you're talking to someone on that long list of audiences we listed earlier. When telling your stories, focus on the donor's *goals*. What difference were they trying to make for your organization and why did they choose that particular asset? If you don't have any stories yet, make some up or borrow from your fundraising friends.

Share Your Successes! We don't do this nearly enough and that's a big shame. When non-cash gifts start happening, tell everyone who will listen. Tell the staff, the board, and the public.

People like being part of a successful enterprise. When they hear of the incredible things being done with non-cash gifts, they'll want to get involved in some way. Maybe that's with their own gift. Maybe that's by volunteering. Maybe it will be applying to work at your organization. If there are staff or board members still a bit scared of non-cash gifts, success stories will go a long way toward bringing them around. When they see the positive effects, the scary parts will seem less intimidating.

Volunteers are one of the biggest opportunities you could have. One reason people volunteer is because they want to help but don't feel like they have the cash necessary to make a big difference. Help your volunteers to understand the many ways they can make a financial contribution. Make sure they know of all the non-cash gift options. They probably have IRAs and may consider a Qualified Charitable Distribution. They may have some appreciated stock or mutual funds to give, but didn't know they could. The possibilities are limitless.

Your **Board of Directors** is a no-brainer. They already feel so close to your organization that they are willing to serve in a leadership role. They're probably willing to make a leadership-type gift as well. It's just a matter of helping them choose the right *type* of asset to donate.

5. Adjust Goals

Goals are great, but rigid adherence to them is irrational. The world changes quickly. Goals you set years ago may not be relevant today. Check in with your goals often and make sure they're still relevant.

Be willing to adjust goals up, down, or sideways. Once you start receiving non-cash gifts, you'll probably want to refine your numerical goals. You may realize you set them too high or too low. My guess is they'll be too low. The value of non-cash gifts you receive in the beginning will likely far exceed your expectations—IF you put the work into developing your program. You may realize that you created goals that are no longer relevant, and you need to pivot sideways to achieve something completely different. For example, you may want to raise money for a certain program, but then a year or two later realize that a different program is really what your community needs now.

Go into the goal-development process expecting these kinds of curveballs. That way, you'll be more able to shift when you need to.

GO FORTH AND FUNDRAISE NON-CASH GIFTS!

You're ready. It's time. You understand the opportunity that non-cash gifts bring. You understand your donor's financial situation. You know what kind of infrastructure you need to build to begin to solicit and accept non-cash gifts. Now it's time to tackle the assets.

The following chapters will walk you through each type of non-cash asset gift with an **easy to understand, 5-step process.** We will take the fear out of non-cash gifts and get you started in quick order.

Each chapter will be broken down into these 5 steps.

1. **Know the Basics**
2. **Ask for the Right Information**
3. **Evaluate for Opportunity and Risk**
4. **Accept or Decline Respectfully**
5. **Manage or Liquidate**

Now, let's get to it!

Chapter 2:
Gifts of Securities

Stock, mutual funds, and exchange traded funds (ETFs) are all *Securities*. Securities make up about 16% of American wealth[4] but only about 7% of the dollars given to charity each year.[5] This is a very significant imbalance, especially since securities are one of the easiest and most advantageous charitable gifts—for the donor and for the charity.

More and more charities are beginning to accept securities on a regular basis. That's probably because it's so easy for both the donor and charity. It's also incredibly beneficial to the charity. Research by Russell James, PhD, revealed that **charities that accept stock and mutual funds experienced 66% growth in total fundraising** over a five-year period.[6]

You'll find *sample* procedures for gifts of stock and mutual funds at the end of this chapter. They are meant to help you get started. You will definitely want to edit them to include your organization's own internal workings.

Now, let's walk through our 5-Step process for gifts of stock, mutual funds, and ETFs.

1. **Know the Basics**
2. **Ask for the Right Information**
3. **Evaluate for Opportunity and Risk**
4. **Accept or Decline Respectfully**
5. **Manage or Liquidate**

---

[4] Federal Census Data, 2008
[5] Aggregate IRS Tax Data, 2012
[6] James, Russell, PhD. "Cash is Not King in Fundraising: Gifts of Non-Cash Assets Predicts Contributions Growth" (2018)

STEP 1: KNOW THE BASICS OF STOCK, MUTUAL FUNDS, AND ETFS

When charities start accepting non-cash gifts, they usually start with publicly traded securities because they're typically the easiest to accept and liquidate.

Before we get into the details on how to accept stock and mutual funds, let's first make sure you understand the difference between public and private stock.

Public stock is available for just about anyone to purchase and it's traded at places like the New York Stock Exchange. When you buy stock in a company you are becoming part owner in that company. **If you want to buy shares of a publicly traded company, you can just go out and buy it.**

Private stock is only bought and sold among a specific group of people—usually members of the same family or a small number of business partners. Unless you're a member of that defined group, the company's rules preclude you from owning it. We will cover privately held stock in detail in Chapter 7.

Mutual funds are also available for virtually anyone to purchase, but they are bought and sold a little differently than stock. **Mutual funds are a collection of investments—such as stocks and bonds—packaged together by a financial services company and sold as a bundle to the consumer.** Mutual funds gained popularity as a way for investors to diversify their investment portfolios without having to spend a great deal of time researching investments. The mutual fund company managers do that for you. Mutual funds are typically only available for purchase from the company that created them and if you want to sell them, you must sell back to the company.

The exception is *Exchange Traded Funds*, or ETFs. They are available to purchase on the stock exchange like stocks. You don't have to go to the mutual fund manufacturing company to buy and sell. You can buy and sell them on the stock exchange.

Nearly all public stock and mutual funds are traded electronically these days. Almost no one is working with paper certificates, but there are still some floating around in safety deposit boxes and desk drawers. You'll need to know how to accept both electronic and certificated shares.

Before you start advertising your ability to accept stock, you'll need to get set up with the right infrastructure. Let's review the necessary setup to accept electronically traded stock and ETFs.

The first step to accepting stock or ETFs is to open a brokerage account. This is sort of like a bank account, but instead of holding just cash, it holds stocks and/or ETFs. This account will allow you to accept and liquidate stock and ETFs electronically. You can open a DIY-type of brokerage account online OR you can hire a broker to handle transactions for you. DIY accounts typically come with fewer transaction fees but offer little to no support service. They operate via online platforms, are easy to access, and are relatively easy to use. A professional broker will usually cost more, but you also receive professional service and support.

When deciding between DIY online account or a professional broker, it's important to consider whether your staff has the time and expertise to manage a brokerage account on a day-to-day basis. Most charities operate under the policy that all non-cash gifts received are sold as soon as possible. That is very important when dealing with stock, because the value can rise and fall very quickly. It's important to be able to monitor your stock account closely so that when gifts are received, you can quickly sell them. **If your staff doesn't have the time or expertise to monitor an account daily, it might be best to hire a professional to handle it for you.** You may have to pay a little more in fees and maintain a minimum account balance, but you reduce your risk of losing value in the stock if the price falls considerably between the time it arrives in your account and the time you sell it.

If you decide to hire a professional broker, it's important to understand all the costs associated with that relationship and to work with someone who understands institutional investing. When you receive and sell stock, your investment policy may require some or all sales proceeds to be reinvested into a board-approved portfolio. **The broker should understand your investment policy and the needs of institutional investors.** It's a best practice to interview a few brokers before choosing one to work with.

If your organization has an endowment fund, it may already be invested with a professional investment manager who can also help you to accept stock and ETF gifts. Your relationship with that manager may already include this service, so getting set up may be even easier than you think.

Most states have adopted The *Uniform Prudent Management of Institutional Funds Act* (UPMIFA).[7] It lays out governing principles and rules for investing endowment funds. If you hire a professional broker to manage your endowment, they should be well-versed in UPMIFA regulations.

A gift of publicly traded securities is one of the most financially beneficial gifts that someone could make. When you give stock or mutual funds, the income tax deduction is based on the fair market value of the shares on the day of the gift, regardless of what you paid for it (as long as it's been owned for at least a year and a day). Simply put, if you paid $5.00 for a share of stock 10 years ago and today it's worth $25.00, your deduction for a gift of that share of stock would be $25.00. That's basically $20.00 of deduction for FREE! Additionally, you avoid recognition of the capital gain when the gift is made. That means you don't have to pay capital gains tax like you would if you sold the stock. When it comes to charitable deductions, not all assets receive this special treatment. Only long-term capital assets like securities qualify for this exceptional double benefit.

---

[7] https://www.uniformlaws.org/committees/community-home?CommunityKey=043b9067-bc2c-46b7-8436-07c9054064a3

If you sell the stock and donate the cash, you don't avoid the capital gains tax. Sure, you would be entitled to a charitable income tax deduction for the cash gift, but that extra capital gains income can cause a ripple effect in your tax picture. For example, extra income can increase the tax paid on Social Security income or increase Medicare premiums. Charitable deductions don't have any effect on those increased expenses. In the end, it's much more efficient to give the stock itself.

The deduction for a gift of publicly traded securities is equal to the average of the high and low trade values on the day the charity receives the shares.

If someone owns securities, their portfolio is probably worth more than their checking and savings accounts combined. People don't keep a lot of money in cash anymore. According to that same research by Russell James, PhD, referenced in Chapter 1, cash makes up less than 3% of America's wealth. Interest rates are historically low and have been for a long time. It makes more sense to invest extra cash in something other than a cash account earning almost nothing. When you ask for a gift of securities, it's coming from a much bigger pot than if you ask for a gift of cash. A gift from that pot is much less painful for the donor, because they have more of it than they do cash.

STEP 2: ASK FOR THE RIGHT INFORMATION

Before accepting any non-cash gift, you want to know as much as you can about what you're getting. So, you'll want to request some information to help you decide whether it's something you want to receive.

Develop a securities gift instruction document you can share with donors and their advisors. This document tells a donor and her advisors *exactly* how to make these gifts to your organization. Below are some items to consider including in your instruction document.

Notify your organization that the gift is coming. Tell the donor *exactly who to contact at your organization and how.* Ask them to share:
1. How many shares they wish to donate,
2. How long they've owned the shares, and
3. The "ticker symbol" of those shares, OR the name and class of mutual fund.

Length of ownership matters because the donor is entitled to a charitable deduction equal to fair market value only if the shares have been held for at least a year and a day. If so, they are considered "long-term capital gain" property. If not, they are considered "short-term capital gain" property and the deduction is limited to their basis (what they paid for the shares).

The ticker symbol is a unique identifying code used to distinguish stocks from each other. You may want to include a section on the back side of the instruction sheet where the donor can write/type in the number of shares and ticker symbol. They can then send that document to you as notification of their intended gift.

Sample Securities Gift Instructions and *Securities Questionnaire* can be found at the end of this chapter. These documents are meant to get you started. You will want to edit them to meet your organization's specific needs.

STEP 3: EVALUATE FOR OPPORTUNITY AND RISK

The biggest risks with accepting any non-cash gift are expenses and liabilities that arise between acceptance and sale. Publicly traded securities come with virtually no risk because they cost virtually nothing to own, and I've not yet run into a case where they exposed a charity to legal liability. You still may want to evaluate the stock before you accept it.

One thing to consider is whether the stock is from a company that poses ethical issues for your organization. For instance, the company may manufacture products that conflict with your charitable mission. There are two schools of thought when it comes to this situation. First, you could decline the gift to avoid engaging at all with the company in question. Second, you could accept the gift, sell the stock, and use the proceeds for your mission that works in opposition to that company's products or services.

There may be other reasons you don't want to accept a particular stock, mutual fund, or ETF. In order to uncover those details, you must ask for the information outlined in Step 2, so you know what you're getting.

STEP 4: ACCEPT OR DECLINE RESPECTFULLY

If you decide to accept the securities, provide the donor and/or their advisor with your account information for electronic transfer. Your broker or DIY online account platform can provide you with these instructions. The donor will use those instructions to electronically transfer stock or ETFs into your account. It is a very fast process, and the stock will usually appear in your account within a few days.

If a donor wants to contribute stocks in paper certificate form, it will take a little longer and your procedure will be different.

First, the donor will need to deliver to you both the stock certificates AND a completed *Stock Power Form*. The Stock Power Form indicates to whom the donor is transferring the certificates. They should either hand-deliver these items to you OR send in two separate, trackable packages. Sending the certificates and stock power form in the same package can be risky if someone were to intercept it. It could be possible for them to transfer the shares to themselves by altering the Stock Power Form.

When you receive both the certificates and Stock Power Form, a broker can help you convert the shares from paper to electronic. If you have a DIY online account, their customer service department should be able to help you with this process. Once they've been converted and are held in your electronic account, you can retain the securities or liquidate.

If a donor wants to contribute traditional mutual funds—not ETFs—you'll need to set up an account with the mutual fund company in order to receive the funds from the donor. This can take considerable time and paperwork, so be prepared for that. You'll want to inquire with the mutual fund company as to how quickly you can liquidate the funds. They don't tend to liquidate as fast as stocks, and the value can fluctuate during the time between receipt and sale. Once you have liquidated them, you can transfer the cash proceeds to another account. You can also choose to keep the mutual fund account open for future gifts of funds issued by that company or close it.

No matter the type of gift, it is very important to communicate your gift acceptance process with the donor.

Let them know what you will do with the gift once it's received. It's important to be transparent with donors. If your gift acceptance policies require you to sell immediately and reinvest into a board-approved investment portfolio, make sure you say so. Whatever your intent, let the donor know what will happen to their gift after receipt.

Let them know how/when you will send them a gift receipt. In order to take a tax deduction for a gift of stock, the donor will need a gift receipt from you. That receipt should NOT list the value of the stock, but rather:

- The date of the gift, (day the stock is received in the charity's account)
- The number of shares, and
- Name and/or ticker symbol of the stock/ETF, or name of mutual fund.

It's up to the donor or her tax advisor to report the value of the stock on her tax return.

If you decide to decline the gift, it is VERY important to explain exactly WHY. People don't like to hear the word "no". Donors can feel especially offended if they offer a gift and you decline without an explanation. If a donor really cares about your organization, they will understand why you've declined their gift. You need only to take the time to explain. It's a good idea to do this verbally and accompany your conversation with a written explanation. The gift may not be 100% lost. For example, if you explain that you cannot accept the stock for ethical reasons that violate your gift acceptance policies, the donor may offer to make a gift of a different stock that does not conflict with your mission.

As I stated earlier, publicly traded securities come with little to no risk. You will rarely need to decline one of these gifts.

STEP 5: MANAGE OR LIQUIDATE

Most charities liquidate all non-cash assets as soon as possible. If you fall into this camp and want to liquidate stock or mutual funds you've received, it is very easy. Stock and ETFs can typically be liquidated within 24 hours of receipt. Traditional mutual funds take longer, but the process is still simple. If you work with a broker, she can handle liquidation for you. If you have a DIY online account, you can sell quickly with a click of a button. In either case, sales proceeds will usually show up in your account in 1-3 days. From there you can transfer the cash to another account or use it to purchase other investments.

SPECIAL CONSIDERATIONS FOR GIFTS OF SECURITIES TO ESTABLISH A CHARITABLE GIFT ANNUITY OR CHARITABLE REMAINDER TRUST.

Stock, ETFs, and mutual funds can be ideal assets to fund both Charitable Gift Annuities (CGAs) and Charitable Remainder Trusts (CRTs).

They are easy to value and easy to liquidate. These are both very beneficial qualities when establishing a CGA or CRT.

The quick turnaround time between receipt and sale minimizes the risk when issuing a CGA or establishing a Charitable Remainder Annuity Trust (CRAT). The payout amount to the income beneficiary(ies) for both the CGA and CRAT is based on the value of the gift—not the sales proceeds. This means that if sold immediately, the value of the gift is going to be close to the sales proceeds.

Charitable Remainder Unitrusts can accept a very wide array of assets, including stock, ETFs, and mutual funds. The annual payout amount to the income beneficiary(ies) is based on the value of the trust assets each year—not the gift value. This means that the sales proceeds amount is less of a concern. It's still a best practice to liquidate the assets immediately upon receipt and invest in a diversified portfolio. This will reduce the likelihood of significant loss due to market volatility.

The bottom line is you probably can't go wrong funding a CGA, CRAT, or CRUT with a gift of publicly traded stock, ETFs, or mutual funds.

Sample Securities Gift Procedures

1. Conduct initial conversations with donor about their goals and gift basics.

2. Donor completes and returns the *Securities Gift Questionnaire.*

3. Review completed *Securities Gift Questionnaire.*

4. If any red flags arise from review of *Securities Gift Questionnaire,* resolve, if possible.

5. If no red flags exist and gift meets the minimum, work with donor to execute transfer of ownership to charity.
    a. If securities are held electronically, they should be able to be transferred electronically to charity's account.
    b. If securities are held in certificate form, donor will need to execute a Stock Power form and deliver to charity along with the certificates. Donor should *either* hand-deliver to charity OR send in separate trackable overnight delivery packages. For security purposes, Stock Power forms and stock certificates should NOT be sent in the same package.
    c. If donating mutual funds, charity will most likely need to open an account with that mutual fund company to accept.

6. When securities are received by charity, send donor a written acknowledgment of the gift.

Sample Securities Gift Instructions

Donors should consult their tax and legal advisors prior to making a gift to fully understand all financial and tax consequences.

Donors should carefully follow the steps outlined below to protect any potential tax benefits of making the gift.

Steps to Making a Gift of Securities
1. Donor completes the *Securities Gift Questionnaire* and returns to charity.
2. Charity reviews the *Securities Gift Questionnaire* and contacts donor to coordinate asset transfer.
3. Securities transfer to charity.
4. Charity will send a written acknowledgment of the gift to donor.

Sample Securities Gift Questionnaire

Please answer the following questions to the best of your ability. Accuracy and thoroughness are vital to the proper care of your gift. Any information you share will be held in the strictest of confidence and only shared with necessary staff, legal, and tax counsel.

Please complete the following information for each type of security you would like to donate.

Name	Ticker Symbol	Number of Shares	Length of Ownership	Electronic or Certificate?	Approx. Current Value per Share

Please share the name and contact information for your investment broker (if applicable).

_____

Please contact us right away with any questions or concerns you have about this questionnaire. We want you to be absolutely comfortable with your proposed gift. We also want to create an open conversation with you and your advisors about why this information is needed and how it will be used.

I understand that the truth and accuracy of my answers to the previous questions will be relied upon when evaluating my proposed gift of securities. I certify that each of the answers is true, accurate, and complete to the best of my knowledge.

_____   _____

Signature   Date

_____   _____

Print name   Phone Number

Chapter 3:
Gifts of Retirement Assets

This chapter is a bit of an oddball because charitable gifts from a retirement account come in the form of a check. It's not a non-cash asset when the charity receives it, but it does come with its fair share of complexity. Accepting charitable gifts of retirement assets is relatively easy. **The hard part is navigating the complexities that come with retirement accounts themselves.**

There are three primary ways that people give retirement assets:
1. *Qualified Charitable Distributions*
2. *Beneficiary Proceeds*
3. *Testamentary Charitable Remainder Trust funded with Retirement Assets*

We're going to apply our 5-Step process a little differently in this chapter. First, we'll go through some background information and then apply Steps 1-5 to *each* of these three giving methods. I think this approach will help us make sense of the complexities of retirement asset gifts. Here are the 5 steps:

1. **Know the Basics**
2. **Ask for the Right Information**
3. **Evaluate for Opportunity and Risk**
4. **Accept or Decline Respectfully**
5. **Manage or Liquidate**

A BIT OF BACKGROUND

Over the past few decades, Americans have gotten really good at putting money away for retirement. In fact, **the 2011 U.S. Census Data estimates that retirement accounts make up 30% of the wealth of the average American household.** Furthermore, the Investment Company Institute reports that retirement assets in America reached an all-time high of $34.9 trillion at the end of 2020. In the year 2000, that number was $11.6 trillion.[8]

Before the 1980s, company pensions were the norm. People worked at a single company their entire lives and were rewarded with a pension when they retired. Over time, companies discontinued their pension programs and individuals became responsible for their own retirement savings.

The Federal tax code offers special incentives for us to save our money in special "qualified" retirement accounts, such as IRAs, 401(k)s, 403(b)s, etc. **A "qualified" retirement account allows for contributions of pre-tax, earned income.** Pre-tax money is money you've earned but haven't yet paid tax on. If you have a retirement account at work, you probably deposit money into it from each paycheck. Those deposits are made before any income taxes are paid.

Depositing pre-tax money allows us to deposit more money so that there is more to be invested and grow. **Taxes on the contributions and investment growth are deferred until a withdrawal is made.**

Distributions from retirement accounts are taxed at ordinary income tax rates. That is often our highest tax rate (as opposed to capital gains tax rates that are typically lower).

The law also encourages us to leave that money alone to grow until we reach at least 59 1/2 years of age. Lawmakers determined that 59 1/2 is an acceptable retirement age for us. If we withdraw money before 59 1/2, we are taxed on the distribution amount *and* are assessed a 10% penalty on the withdrawn amount. The ordinary income tax plus the 10% penalty can be very steep. There are a few slim exceptions to the 10% penalty, but we won't get into those here.

When we reach age 72, Federal tax law requires that we begin taking *Required Minimum Distributions* (RMDs) from our qualified accounts every year. The minimum distribution amount is determined by a special calculation. That calculation is designed to distribute all the money from the account over the owner's life expectancy. As a result, the older we get, the larger those RMDs tend to be. If we don't take them, we have to pay a 50% penalty on the amount not distributed!

For a variety of reasons, many people defer withdrawals from retirement accounts as long as they can and only take the RMD. They probably want to defer

---

[8] ici.org

withdrawing those highly taxed dollars as long as possible. This deferral allows the accounts to grow larger and larger, year after year. I've seen RMDs in the six and sometimes seven-digit range. Many people have been living a comfortable retirement on pensions, other assets, and Social Security. When RMDs come due at age 72, it can be a big surprise and result in a LOT more taxable income. These large RMDs are very important when it comes to Qualified Charitable Distribution gifts.

Qualified Charitable Distributions

STEP 1: KNOW THE BASICS OF QCDs

A QCD is a distribution from an Individual Retirement Account (IRA) *directly* to a public charity. A Qualified Charitable Distribution:
- is exempt from income tax
- is not deductible
- can count toward a Required Minimum Distribution
- can be made by someone 70.5 years of age or older
- can be up to $100,000 per year per IRA owner (That means a couple can give up to $200,000 per year if they both own IRAs.)

QCDs can only be made from IRAs—not other kinds of retirement accounts such as 401(k)s, 403(b)s, etc. If someone has money in one of those other types of retirement accounts, they can usually transfer it into an IRA without any tax consequences and then make a QCD if they're at least 70 1/2. In fact, after people leave a job or retire, they almost always will "roll" those accounts into an IRA.

Believe it or not, Required Minimum Distributions from retirement accounts are often in the tens or hundreds of thousands of dollars per year. That's right—people are often required to distribute $10,000, $50,000, $200,000 or more from their IRAs each year. **They don't always want or need all that money.** If they're 70.5 or older, they can avoid that extra taxable income by directing those distributions to charity in the form of a QCD.

STEP 2: ASK FOR THE RIGHT INFORMATION ABOUT QCDs

Most of the time when a charity receives a QCD check from an IRA administrator it does NOT indicate the name of the donor. It's completely anonymous and if you call to inquire about the donor's name you'll be met with stony silence. They will not release that information to you because of client privacy rules and policies. Now you're faced with a real conundrum. You want to thank your donor and to know how they would like the money to be used, but you don't know who they are. **You can prevent this problem from occurring by asking the donor for some simple information *before* the**

gift is made. Whenever you're talking to a donor about a QCD—in person, in print, or on your website—make sure you tell them how important it is that they contact you *before* they make the gift. Let them know that the check you receive will NOT include their name, nor will the administrator disclose it to you if you ask.

Provide a simple form for them to complete that includes the following information:
- Their name
- The gift amount
- The name of the IRA Administrator

I don't recommend making this an online form. You don't want that information falling into the wrong hands. Hopefully, with this information ahead of time, you'll be able to match incoming checks with donor names.

In addition, you'll want to make it *really easy* for donors to make a QCD gift to your organization. Spell out the instructions on your website and in email communications. You'll want to share:
- Simple explanation of what a QCD is
- Tax basics of a QCD
- Step-by-step instructions about how to make a QCD gift to your organization.
- Your organization's legal name.
- Your organization's legal address.
- Your organization's Federal Tax ID Number

STEP 3: EVALUATE FOR OPPORTUNITY AND RISK OF QCDs

There is virtually zero risk to accepting a gift in the form of a Qualified Charitable Distribution; however, there is a TON of opportunity.

According to FreeWill, Qualified Charitable Distribution (QCD) gifts increased by 67% from 2018 to 2019. In 2021, they determined that 43% of the donors in survey respondents' databases were over the age of 70.[9]

Donors over the age of 70 1/2 are increasingly making annual gifts from their IRAs, rather than their checking accounts. **This is wonderful news, because their checking accounts are a fraction of the size of their IRAs.**

---

[9] 2021 FreeWill QCD Report, www.freewill.com

PRO TIP

Consider adding "Qualified Charitable Distribution" as a giving option in addition to "Check" and "Credit Card" to your annual fund mailer.

STEP 4: ACCEPT OR DECLINE A QCD RESPECTFULLY

It's not likely that you'd want to decline a QCD gift. If you must decline, you can simply return the check to the IRA administrator with a letter stating that you've chosen not to accept the gift. It's also a good idea to inform the donor that you're declining the gift and why—if you can determine who that donor is. As we discovered above, QCD checks most often arrive to your mailbox with no indication of the donor's name.

After you've accepted a QCD gift, be sure to thank your donor profusely and follow up with her the next summer or fall to see if she wants to make another QCD gift. According to FreeWill, 53% of QCD donors in 2020 had made a QCD gift previously.[10] For most people, **Required Minimum Distributions (RMDs) must be taken by December 31st each year. So, it's a good idea to talk to your donors early in the year to remind them that they can avoid the unwanted income tax associated with their RMD by sending some or all of it (up to $100,000) your way.**

Gift receipts for Qualified Charitable Distribution gifts require special language for the gift to qualify as a tax-exempt distribution from the donor's IRA. I encourage you to consult with your legal counsel to make sure your gift receipt language contains the required elements. This is another reason it is imperative that donors inform you of their QCD. The check you receive probably won't disclose the donor's name. If the donor wants a gift receipt, they will have to alert you to the gift themselves.

STEP 5: MANAGE OR LIQUIDATE THE QCD

Since these gifts come to you in the form of a check, there is no management or liquidation necessary. Simply deposit the check into your account and enjoy the bounty.

Beneficiary Designations

STEP 1: KNOW THE BASICS OF BENEFICIARY DESIGNATIONS

When someone dies, her retirement accounts pass to heirs or to charity according to what's called a "Beneficiary Designation". These accounts are not distributed via probate and are not subject to the terms of someone's Will. Sometimes

---

[10] 2021 FreeWill QCD Report, www.freewill.com

people will designate their estate or a trust as the beneficiary of their retirement accounts. When retirement accounts are established, the owner will be asked to name a beneficiary or beneficiaries. They often name charity to receive some or all of the account balance.

Naming a charity as a beneficiary of a retirement account is just about the easiest gift anyone can make. The donor completes a form and submits it to their account administrator. She can name the charity as the sole beneficiary or a percentage beneficiary. She can also change the beneficiary(ies) at any time by submitting a new beneficiary form to the administrator.

During life, people use these accounts to support themselves in retirement. When they've passed, the money has to be distributed to a new owner. **If given to family and/or friends, those human beneficiaries have to withdraw all the money within 10 years and it's virtually all taxable at their highest income tax rate.**[11] If a charity receives that money, they pay no income tax.

Donors are getting smart about which assets to give to family and which ones to give to charity. They're giving the high-tax assets, like retirement accounts, to charity. They're giving the tax-fee assets, like life insurance, to family and friends.

Given the size of these accounts, it is utterly essential that charities talk to their supporters about naming them as beneficiaries of their retirement accounts. Beneficiary Designation gifts are often the largest gifts that people ever make. You'll want to make it VERY EASY for a donor to name your organization as beneficiary of her retirement account. To do so, she will need the following information:

- Legal name of organization
- Official mailing address of organization
- Federal Tax ID Number of organization

Consider posting this information on your website in an easy-to-find place. Many organizations miss out on big gifts from retirement assets because they don't make this information easy to find. You may also consider creating a simple print piece about gifts from retirement assets and include this vital data about your organization. That way, you can leave it with a donor at a meeting or email it to them or their advisors.

Unfortunately, it's become increasingly difficult for charities to collect beneficiary designation gifts from retirement accounts. It can take more than 18 months to collect money from a retirement account administrator. According to a recent

---

[11] *There are some exceptions to the 10-year rule, but we won't address them in this book.*

survey by the National Association of Charitable Gift Planners, 43% of charities experience difficulty collecting beneficiary proceeds from retirement account administrators.[12] Here's why.

Many administrators treat charities like people when it comes to inheriting retirement assets. Federal rules require investment companies to "know their customers" really, really well. To avoid money laundering, the Patriot Act requires financial firms to collect a LOT of vital data on investors before they're allowed to open accounts or receive distributions from the accounts of others.

The reality is that administrations aren't required by law to collect this same level of information from charities—but they do it anyway. They require the charity to disclose personal information about members of their leadership team and/or board of directors before the money will be released. They often require home addresses, Social Security Numbers, and more. This is unreasonable because these individuals are not receiving the money. Their employer (the charity) is.

To make things worse, charities are often required to open *Inherited Individual Retirement Accounts* of their own before they can have access to the money their donor wanted them to have. I find this absurd because the charity isn't an *Individual* and they aren't ever going to *Retire*. Therefore, it's inappropriate for a charity to open an *Individual Retirement Account*.

Thankfully, some very dedicated and experienced volunteers have given countless hours of their time to try to end these absurd practices. They have created the RIFT Project (*Release IRA Funds Timely*). As a part of this project, the volunteers have created some *very* powerful resources, including step-by-step instructions, customized letters, and more to help you reduce the amount of time and effort it takes to collect gifts from retirement account administrators. **These resources *really work* and are free.** They can be found on the National Association of Charitable Gift Planners website.[13]

STEP 2: ASK FOR THE RIGHT INFORMATION ABOUT THE BENEFICIARY DESIGNATION

First, you'll want to know the *estimated* value of the gift. Most of the time, your organization will be named a percentage beneficiary. The ultimate gift amount depends upon the account balance when the donor passes away. The donor or her wealth advisor should be able to run a projection to estimate the value of the gift at the end of her life expectancy. This information is really helpful if the gift is to be used for a specific purpose. You want to make sure the amount is sufficient to carry out that specific purpose (such as naming a building or providing a scholarship). It's quite possible that the gift

---

[12] https://charitablegiftplanners.org/ira-distribution-resource-center
[13] https://charitablegiftplanners.org/ira-distribution-resource-center

may be a great deal more or less than estimated. For that reason, it's important to talk to the donor about an alternative purpose for the funds.

Second, you'll want to know what company administers the account. When the donor passes away, you will need to know who to contact to collect the funds. Over time, the donor may move the account from one administrator to another. This is one of the reasons donor stewardship is so important. You need to keep in contact with the donor on a regular basis to make sure the information you have about their gift is current. Wealth advisors review beneficiary designations with their clients on a regular basis to make sure the information is still in line with their wishes. It's a best practice for you to do the same.

Third, you'll want to know who will be handling the donor's estate. It's important that the donor's executor knows about the gift and that you know who they are. They will need to notify you of the donor's passing and probably provide you with a certified death certificate. Most of the time, you'll be required to submit a certified copy of the death certificate to the account administrator along with the beneficiary claim form. Sometimes you can get a death certificate from the funeral home, but it may not be a certified copy.

All of this information is likely to change over a donor's lifetime. Her account will grow and diminish over time. She may change account administrators, and she may name a new executor for her estate. She may also delete your organization as a beneficiary. It is vital that you keep in contact with these kinds of donors to:

- Remind them of the value of the gift they are planning; and
- To make sure you have the most current details about the gift.

STEP 3: EVALUATE THE BENEFICIARY DESIGNATION FOR OPPORTUNITY AND RISK

I can't think of any risk that comes with accepting a beneficiary designation gift from a retirement account. The asset comes to you in the form of a check, so it's easy to manage and doesn't come with legal liabilities or other kinds of risk.

This is a very long-haul kind of gift, but you will be rewarded with enormous opportunity. Your organization won't receive the money for a while—possibly many decades. That being said, these gifts are very often enormous. You can think of them as retirement accounts for your organization. You invest your time and energy into cultivating this donor relationship and are rewarded with a six, seven, or eight-figure gift down the road. Just imagine how that could change your organization when the gift is realized. Also imagine what would happen if you realized several of these gifts every...single...year.

STEP 4: ACCEPT OR DECLINE THE BENEFICIARY DESIGNATION RESPECTFULLY

If you choose to decline the gift, you'll want to let the estate executor and the account administrator know that you won't be filing a claim to collect the funds. They will want something in writing to this effect. After you decline the gift, the assets can be sent by the administrator to the contingent beneficiary(ies) named on the account.

As we outlined above, acceptance should be simple, but often it's not. Once you learn of the donor's passing, you'll need to file a certified copy of the death certificate with the account administrator. They may ask you to open an *Inherited IRA* before you can receive the money, but I advise you to push back against that requirement. It's time-consuming and invasive. Instead, use the resources provided by the *RIFT Project* (described above) to avoid those additional hoops and get your money faster.

Gift receipts for a gift of Beneficiary Proceeds are typically sent to the estate administrator. They will need it to substantiate a charitable estate tax deduction. That might be a Personal Representative, Executor, or Trustee. I encourage you to reach out to whomever is administering the estate to find out where they would like the receipt sent and to whom to address it.

STEP 5: MANAGE OR LIQUIDATE THE BENEFICIARY DESIGNATION

Since these gifts come to you in the form of a check, there is no management or liquidation necessary. Simply deposit the check into your account and enjoy the bounty.

Testamentary Charitable Remainder Trust (TCRT) Funded with Retirement Assets

STEP 1: KNOW THE BASICS ABOUT TCRTs

This giving technique is not new, but it is receiving renewed interest due to recent legislation that limits the payout period from inherited IRAs to 10 years for most people.[14]

First off, we need to make sure we understand the basics of a Charitable Remainder Trust (CRT). **A CRT is a tax-exempt trust that provides income to people for their lifetimes, a period of up to 20 years, or a combination of both, and then the remaining assets are distributed to charity.** CRTs can be established during life or at death. **"Testamentary" means "at death".** They can take the form of *either* a Charitable Remainder Unitrust (CRUT) OR a Charitable Remainder Annuity Trust (CRAT). The main difference is that a CRUT provides a variable income stream to the

---

[14] *Setting Every Community Up for Retirement Enhancement Act of 2019* (SECURE)

income beneficiaries and the CRAT provides a fixed income stream to the income beneficiaries.

If funded during life, the donor is entitled to an income tax charitable deduction for the expected amount going to charity. If funded at death, the donor is entitled to an estate tax charitable deduction for the expected amount going to charity. If the CRT is to be funded at death, the donor's attorney will place the language for the CRT *within* the donor's existing Will or Living Trust. **The Testamentary CRT cannot stand alone. It must "live" within the donor's estate documents.**

Let's say I want to provide an income stream to loved ones after I die, and I also want to provide a nice charitable gift. **A Testamentary CRT is designed to accomplish both of those goals.** A donor can contribute virtually any asset to a CRT. In this example, I'm going to donate my IRA to the CRT by naming it as the beneficiary of the IRA. After my passing, the CRT trustee collects the IRA assets, places them in the trust and begins making payments to the loved ones I've named in the CRT document. I'd like them to receive payments for 20 years. Whatever is left after 20 years is to be sent to my favorite charities. That 20-year payment period to my loved ones is what has created a renewed interest in the testamentary CRT.

The SECURE Act limits the amount of time someone must withdraw the balance of an *inherited* IRA to 10 years.[15] Before the SECURE Act, you could withdraw the balance of an *inherited* IRA over your lifetime. Now, most people only have 10 years. IRA distributions are typically 100% taxable at your highest income tax rate. That means you could be forced to withdraw a lot more taxable income than you want/need. This is where the Testamentary CRT can be helpful.

In my example, I've used my IRA beneficiary proceeds to fund my Testamentary CRT and decided that the human beneficiaries of that trust will receive payments for 20 years following my death. If I'd left the IRA directly to my heirs, they would be forced to withdraw the entire amount in no more than 10 years. They would also have access to the entire account balance at any time and could withdraw it all at any time. Naming the CRT as beneficiary of the IRA they will receive payments over 20 years and only have access to their payments—not the corpus of the trust. After those 20 years, whatever is left in the trust will be distributed to the charities I designated in the CRT agreement. **This is a very attractive solution for people who want to "stretch out" the payments to loved ones over a period of time AND make a charitable gift.**

This solution can also be attractive if I want to make sure my heirs don't withdraw all the money right away. It took me my entire working life to accumulate that money. I don't want them to spend it all right away. I want it to last. I also like that the corpus of the trust isn't subject to my heirs' creditors—nor will it be included in any divorce settlements.

---

[15] *There are a few exceptions to the 10-year rule, but we won't address them in this book.*

Their payments from the CRT could be garnished, but the corpus and the ultimate gift to charity is protected.

STEP 2: ASK FOR THE RIGHT INFORMATION ABOUT THE TCRT

There is very little you will need to do to collect this gift in the future, so the information you'll need to gather is mainly for informational purposes.

When the donor passes away, the CRT trustee will collect the beneficiary proceeds from the account administrator. They will invest that money and make the payments to the human beneficiaries.

When the trust comes to its scheduled end, the trustee will distribute your organization's portion of the trust remainder. They will likely contact you when that time comes to have you sign a receipt and to inquire as to exactly how to send the money to you—check, electronic transfer, etc.

For your purposes, you'll want to collect the following information at the time the trust agreement is written into the donor's estate documents:

- *Estimated* value of your portion of the remainder,
- Name of the donor's estate administrator,
- Payment term to the human beneficiaries,
- Name and contact information for the trustee, and
- A copy of the CRT agreement—if possible.

The value of both the donor's retirement account and CRT can fluctuate up and down quite a bit over the years, but the donor's advisors and/or the CRT trustee should be able to run an estimated calculation to determine what your organization's portion of the trust remainder might be.

The donor may change her estate administrator over the years, so you'll want to keep in contact and make sure your data is up to date. You'll definitely want to know when the donor passes away and the IRA administrator should know about this gift.

The payment term to the human beneficiaries begins to run when the donor passes away. The term could be lifetime(s), a term of years up to 20, OR lifetime(s) plus a term of years up to 20. The payment term is defined by the donor and written into the CRT agreement.

The trustee named in the CRT agreement is not likely to change, but it can. The donor may reserve the right to change the trustee during her life OR the trustee can resign and nominate a new trustee. Whatever the case, it's best if you know who the trustee is, because you may want to ask them for a value projection from time to time. This can help greatly with your own budget projections. You'll also want to simply know who will be sending you the remainder gift when the trust ends.

It's a very good practice to request a copy of the CRT agreement. The donor and/or her advisors may be reluctant to share the entire document with you because they may want to keep some information private—such as the names of the human beneficiaries and the other charitable remainder beneficiaries. If that's the case, you could request a written description of the vital information listed above. They should be willing to share that with you, since your organization is a remainder beneficiary of the TCRT.

STEP 3: EVALUATE THE TCRT FOR OPPORTUNITY AND RISK

This is a very long-haul kind of gift. Your organization won't receive the money for a while—possibly decades. Despite the time commitment, these gifts are very often enormous. You can think of them as retirement accounts for your organization. You invest your time and energy into cultivating this donor relationship and are rewarded with a six, seven, or eight-figure gift down the road. Just imagine how that could change your organization when the gift is realized.

One risk that is associated with this gift comes up when charities serve as the *trustee* of a Charitable Remainder Trust. Some charities do this as a matter of practice, but you should be aware of the risks. A trustee is responsible for many things, including:

- Asset management and investment
- Annual tax filings
- Payments to human income beneficiaries
- Protecting assets for the human and charitable beneficiary

Litigation is not uncommon. The human or charitable beneficiaries may feel the trustee has mismanaged the assets or misreported data on the tax filings and could file a lawsuit. Furthermore, these are *tax-exempt* trusts. The IRS keeps a very close eye on them.

A trustee is considered a *fiduciary*. Fiduciaries have a *legal* duty to protect the interests of those they are charged with protecting. In this case, it's the human and charitable beneficiaries. Violation of that duty could result in severe penalties for the trustee as an organization or for the individual at the organization who is in charge of managing the trust.

Think twice before agreeing to serve as trustee of a Charitable Remainder Trust. Understand all the risks and get professional legal guidance before you do it.

STEP 4: ACCEPT OR DECLINE THE TCRT GIFT RESPECTFULLY

When the trust comes to its scheduled end, the trustee will contact your organization to let you know that the charitable remainder is ready to be distributed. They will likely require you to sign a receipt for the money before sending you a check or wiring the funds to your account.

It is a rare case when a charity declines the charitable remainder from a CRT. If you choose to decline, the trustee will ask you to do so in writing so they can redistribute your portion to any other charitable beneficiaries named in the trust. If there are none, it will likely fall to the trustee to choose one or more to receive the funds.

Gift receipts for a gift of the remainder of a Charitable Remainder Trust should be sent to the trustee of the CRT. This is another reason it is important to know who the trustee is and how to contact them.

STEP 5: MANAGE OR LIQUIDATE THE TCRT GIFT

Since these gifts come to you in the form of a check, there is no management or liquidation necessary. Simply deposit the check into your account and enjoy the bounty.

Chapter 4:
Gifts of Real Estate

Real estate makes up approximately 30% of American wealth[16] but comprises less than 2% of the total dollars given to charity annually.[17] That is a HUGE imbalance. Why does this happen? In my experience it's because:

- *Charities don't ask for gifts of real estate.*
- *Donors don't know they can give real estate.*
- *Advisors don't discuss gifts of real estate with clients.*

Why don't charities ask?

I believe there are four reasons they don't ask. The first is **fear of risks**. Real estate can bring some risk with it, but if you know what to look for, you can identify these risks early on and potentially mitigate them. I will innumerate the potential risks a little later in Step 3, so you know exactly how to deal with them.

The second reason is **lack of understanding**. Most nonprofit staff don't have professional experience dealing with real estate in any way. They may own their own home, but that's as far as their expertise goes.

The third reason is **lack of staff**. Evaluating and managing a complex gift like real estate requires a fair amount of staff time. If your staff is completely swamped doing other jobs, they won't have time to devote to handling gifts that require time and attention. The step-by-step procedures and checklists in this book will greatly reduce the amount of time your staff will have to devote to these types of gifts. They will streamline the process and create significant efficiencies for you. Both of which will make you feel and appear extremely professional to donors and their advisors.

---

[16] Federal Reserve Data, 2008
[17] Aggregate IRS tax return data, 2012

The fourth reason is **a bad past experience**. If you've worked in fundraising for any amount of time, you probably have a story about a gift of real estate gone bad OR you've heard a really scary one from someone else. I get it. I have some real doozies I could tell you from my experience, but the vast majority have been great and resulted in six and seven-figured gifts for charity! If you know what speedbumps to look for, you won't often be caught off guard.

Now, let's use our 5-step process to demystify gifts of real estate. I recommend using virtually the same processes for outright gifts of real estate and Life Estate Reserved (LER) gifts. I will note where process may differ for LER Gifts. You'll find two items—a *Sample Real Estate Gift Procedures* (outright and LER) and a *Real Estate Gift Questionnaire*—at the end of this chapter. These documents are meant to get you started. You will want to edit them to account for your organization's unique needs.

1. **Know the Basics**
2. **Ask for the Right Information**
3. **Evaluate for Opportunity and Risk**
4. **Accept or Decline Respectfully**
5. **Manage or Liquidate**

STEP 1: KNOW THE BASICS OF REAL ESTATE

Tax Basics

Real estate is one of the most beneficial assets to give to charity—both for the donor and for the organization. Real estate is a capital gain asset—like stock and mutual funds. Therefore, the same beneficial tax rules apply. The charitable deduction is based on the fair market value of the property at the time of the gift. If it's highly appreciated, the donor can receive a deduction that is much larger than what they paid for the property.

For example, let's assume I own a vacation home with a current value of $350,000 and I bought it 10 years ago for $125,000. If I sold it today, I would recognize $225,000 of capital gains (current value minus purchase price). I will owe capital gains tax on the $225,000 of appreciation. Federal capital gains rates can be as high as 23.8%.[18] If my state assesses capital gains tax, that will increase the tax I must pay.[19]

If I no longer wish to use the vacation home and decide to donate it to charity, I would be entitled to a charitable income tax deduction of the current appraised value of $350,000. That deduction reduces my taxable income by $350,000. If my average federal income tax rate is 25%, that deduction may save me $87,500! Plus, I also avoid all the capital gains tax on the gain—a savings of up to $53,550.

---

[18] *20% capital gains rate + 3.8% Net Investment Income Tax.*
[19] The numbers in this example are simplified for the sake of illustration.

Not all assets receive this same favorable treatment. The charitable deduction for gifts of some assets is limited to basis—the purchase price. And some gifts require the donor to recognize the asset's appreciation before taking a charitable deduction. That isn't nearly as beneficial.

Let's take this example a little further to illustrate another tax tidbit you'll want to know. Federal tax rules limit the amount of <u>capital gains</u> gifts I can deduct to 30% of my *Adjusted Gross Income* (AGI). Let's assume my *AGI* is $100,000. That means my deduction is limited to $30,000 this year. I don't lose the remaining $320,000 of the deduction. I have an additional 5 years to use it up. If I don't, any unused portion will be lost after that 6th year. Many people in this situation will look for ways to increase their income to use more of the deduction sooner. By that same token, many people will decide to make a large gift like this in a year when they have extra income from things like a business sale, exercising stock options, or rebalancing an investment portfolio.

> ***"Taxes don't determine the WHY of the gift, but they very often determine the WHEN of the gift."~ Dana Holt***

There is one more tax tidbit I want you to remember. At the time of this book's publication, capital gain assets left to heirs at someone's death receive a *stepped-up basis*. That means that if I passed away today and left my $350,000 vacation home to my best friend, her basis in the property would be $350,000. She could sell the property right away without recognizing ANY capital gains tax. Remember that formula for determining taxable gain? (Sale price minus basis)

```
  $350,000      sale price
- $350,000      basis
  $0 taxable gain
```

You'll want to note that this special tax treatment does not apply to real estate given to people during the donor's lifetime. During life, a gift of real estate to people results in *carry-over basis*. That means the person receiving the real estate will take on the donor's basis. They don't receive that "step-up" in basis.

What does this have to do with charitable giving? If I have heirs, my real estate can be an ideal asset to give them when I pass away. It minimizes the amount of taxes they will have to pay when selling the real estate. So, don't be surprised if donors are more inclined in some cases to give real estate to their heirs at death and leave other kinds of assets to you. For example, retirement accounts are highly taxable when left to heirs, but charities pay zero tax. You can read all about gifts of retirement accounts in Chapter 3.

By the same token, if someone owns real estate and they want to divest themselves of it during lifetime, a charitable gift can be a great option. Selling it themselves could result in significant capital gains tax. If given to another person, that person receives a *carry-*

over basis and could be subject to significant capital gains tax when they sell. If given to charity, the donor could be entitled to a charitable income tax deduction based on the fair market value AND avoid the capital gains on the appreciated value. Not a bad option to consider.

The charitable deduction for a gift of real estate with Life Estate Reserved (LER) is based on the appraised value and is received during the donor's lifetime. The difference is that the value of the LER is deducted from the value of the gift. Fortunately for us, that value is easily calculated by our gift planning software.

Appraisals

In order to claim a charitable deduction for a gift of real estate, the donor will very likely need to acquire a *Qualified Appraisal* of the property. The requirements for that special type of appraisal are outlined in IRS Publications 526 and 561. Those publications are like instruction manuals for charitable income tax deductions. They are available at IRS.gov and are surprisingly easy to understand. I recommend keeping them on hand for quick reference.

Why does the donor need an appraisal? It's pretty simple. The IRS wants proof that the amount of the deduction is the actual fair market value at the time of the gift.

When the donor files her tax return, she will also need to include IRS Form 8283 along with a copy of the appraisal to substantiate that amount. Form 8283 must be signed by the donor, the appraiser, and the charity. The appraiser attests to have performed the appraisal of the property and the charity attests to have received that same property on a specific date. The charity is NOT attesting to the value. That is never their job. That's what the appraisal is for.

Charities sometimes pay for appraisals for their donors, but *I don't believe that is a good practice*. The appraisal is required of the taxpayer, and it is their obligation to acquire it. It is not a proper use of charitable dollars to satisfy an obligation of a taxpayer. A donor may be able to deduct the cost of the appraisal as a miscellaneous expense on Schedule A of their tax return. If a charity *does* pay for the appraisal, the cost should be noted on the real estate gift receipt as something of value the donor received.

STEP 2: ASK FOR THE RIGHT INFORMATION

At the end of this chapter you'll find a detailed *Sample Real Estate Gift Questionnaire* for a donor to complete. It is meant to get you started. You will want to edit it to meet your organization's specific needs. It covers a great deal of information – both technical and environmental - about the real estate. Here, we'll go through some of the more important types of information you'll want to gather and *why*.

Title

Title is important for two reasons. First, you want to know how the property is *titled*. That refers to who owns the property. Is it owned by a married couple, a business, or a trust? It's always a good idea to know *who* is making the gift.

Second, it's essential that the title is "clean". That means there are no encumbrances that would preclude ownership from being transferred to your organization OR preclude you from selling the property to a buyer. Encumbrances are things like delinquent taxes, mechanic's liens, pending litigation, deceased persons still on the title (I've seen this one several times.). Some encumbrances are easy to fix. Some take years and a lot of money to resolve. The best way to find out the current state of the title is to order a "title commitment" from a title company. We'll look at title in more detail later in Step 3 when we evaluate risks.

Current and Previous Uses of the Property

It's vital for you to know how the property is being used now and how it was used in the past. If the property has been used for something that could cause environmental contamination, you want to know about it. Even if happened many years ago, the contamination could still be lingering on the property and you could be responsible for clean-up costs. More on environmental risks later on in Step 3.

The current use will also affect how easy it will be to sell the property. If there is a tenant renting the property, that could decrease the number of people who want to purchase it. If it is a commercial property (such as a warehouse or office building), the timeline for the gift process is going to be a bit longer. Commercial properties are more complex and require more intricate due diligence on the part of the charity. There will be more details to consider.

Mortgaged Property

What if a donor proposes a gift of real estate, but it has a mortgage on it? It may not be the best asset for that donor to give, because of the *Bargain Sale*[20] rules. That rule requires a donor to recognize income in the amount of the outstanding loan if she donates a mortgaged property to charity. Furthermore, the lender would likely have to agree to the gift, and that may not be an easy thing to arrange. If the lender did agree, your organization would most likely be required to assume the mortgage and be obligated to pay the outstanding debt.

If the donor really wants to donate this property, there are a couple options she can consider. First, she could pay off the mortgage with other assets prior to making the gift. Second, she could transfer the mortgage to a different property. Either way, the property in question should be debt-free before it is given to charity.

---

[20] 26 CFR § 1.1011-2 (a)(3)

Carrying Costs

You'll want to know how much it's going to cost you to own the property. Even if you plan to sell the property soon after the gift is made, there will still be costs of ownership. You'll be responsible for property taxes, maintenance, utilities, insurance, etc.

Value

It is essential that you determine a minimum value for each type of non-cash gift, especially real estate. Gifts of real estate require considerable time, attention, and expertise. Therefore, you want to make sure that the value of the property is worth the resources you will expend to evaluate, accept, manage, and/or liquidate it. It is a very good practice to list this minimum value in your gift acceptance policies and be sure those policies are reviewed regularly—at least every 3 years.

How do you assess the value without an appraisal? The tax-assessed value is often a good way to determine relative value. You could also engage a real estate broker to give you an estimated sale price. Many times, they will do that for little to no cost.

You may want to establish different minimums for different types of realestate, such as residential, commercial, farm, and vacant land. Residential property is often less complicated to deal with than commercial. Therefore, your minimum for residential property could be much less than that of commercial property.

Setting minimums in advance allows you to quickly determine whether a proposed gift is something you may want to accept or not. By listing the minimums in your policies, it doesn't fall to one or a few people to make that decision every time a gift is proposed. It is an official policy of the organization and not a random decision. That being said, I do think it is a good idea to give yourself the flexibility to make exceptions to those policies when it makes sense. For example, someone may propose a gift of a condominium that doesn't quite meet your minimum for residential real estate. The market analysis may show that the property is likely to sell very quickly. The condo management staff may be very adept, which means you'll have little to no maintenance costs for the property while it's up for sale.

Bottom line—your risks appear to be low and therefore it might be prudent to waive your gift minimum in that case. Policies are essential, but sometimes it's in your best interest to be able to make an exception.

Acquisition Date

If the donor has owned the property less than a year and a day, the property is going to be considered *short-term capital gain property*, rather than *long-term*. That's important for deductibility reasons. If the property is *short-term*, the donor's deduction is limited to her basis. If it's *long-term*, the deduction is based on the fair market value of the property as discussed above.

Pending Sale

Sometimes donors wait too long before exploring the idea of donating a piece of real estate. They put the property on the market, receive an offer and accept it. Only then does someone suggest that they could donate the property, receive a charitable income tax deduction, and avoid the capital gains tax on the sale. They come to you proposing to donate the property and tell you they already have a buyer lined up. That may sound like an ideal situation, but wait—it may not be.

If a donor is already obligated to sell the property to someone else and they donate it to you instead, they are in breach of their agreement to sell to that other person. Furthermore, if they donate the property to your organization and then you sell to that buyer according to the terms of the deal they already negotiated, that's a prearranged sale. It doesn't really affect the charity, but it could negatively affect the donor.

If the IRS discovers a prearranged sale, the donor could very likely be required to recognize the capital gains on the sale of the property even though they weren't the ones who sold it. Your organization sold the property and received the sales proceeds. The donor would likely still be able to claim a charitable income tax deduction for a cash gift equal to the sales proceeds, but as we discussed above, it's not nearly as advantageous to the donor.

If someone comes to you and proposes a gift with a buyer all lined up, be careful. It's best to have the donor and the buyer cancel any purchase agreement they have negotiated (written or oral) before the gift is made. After the gift is made, your organization will negotiate an arm's-length transaction with a buyer.

Pre-arrangement can be a very gray area. The laws aren't in complete agreement as to exactly what constitutes pre-arrangement. You shouldn't try to advise a donor as to whether they have engaged in pre-arrangement. That is best left to experienced legal counsel. If you suspect pre-arrangement, it's best to bring it up with the donor and strongly encourage them to consult experienced legal counsel before proceeding with the gift.

STEP 3: EVALUATE FOR OPPORTUNITY AND RISK

This is going to be the most important step in the process. It requires close attention to detail, and it can be time-consuming. Below I'll go through some of the most important considerations when evaluating a gift of real estate.

You'll never be able to eliminate all risks, but if you do a thorough investigation of the property, you'll know what you're dealing with. You can minimize surprises and be able to quantify the risks before you accept the gift.

Marketability + Carrying Costs

This is probably the biggest risk when accepting real estate—how long will it take to sell? No one can say for sure how long a property will take to sell. Virtually all real estate comes with expenses, and the longer you own a property, the more expenses you'll have to cover. Here is a list of some common expenses you'll incur.

- Property taxes
- Property insurance
- Utilities
- Outdoor maintenance (lawn, snow-removal, landscaping, etc.)

If a market analysis shows the property is likely to take several months or even years to sell, you may consider asking the donor to contribute several months or years worth of expenses in cash to cover those costs. Otherwise, it's going to eat into your organization's cash flow. If a donor really cares for your organization, they will understand if you can't afford to cover those costs for an extended period of time. Hopefully, they will be willing and able to help cover these carrying costs. If not, you may want to consider declining the gift for the time being and suggesting the donor consider making the gift when the property is likely to sell more quickly.

Don't try to cut corners on carrying costs. Make sure you carry the proper insurance, pay the property taxes, and maintain the buildings and grounds.

I once worked on a gift of a small apartment building. Between the time the gift was received and the time we sold it, the building caught fire, the sewer backed up, asbestos was discovered, and tenants had to be relocated during clean-up and repairs. Thankfully, we carried the right amount of insurance because repairs cost over $75,000. I'm also thankful we hired a very diligent property manager for this property.

Tenants

What if a donor wants to donate a property that is currently rented by a tenant? This is very common. I've worked on many gifts like this. There are a few things you'll want to know when considering a rented property.

First, when someone donates a rented property, the lease comes with it and your organization becomes the new landlord. The lease doesn't automatically terminate when ownership changes hands. Are you comfortable being a landlord and taking care of things like maintenance, collecting rents, carrying proper insurance? If not, I highly recommend hiring an experienced property manager to take good care of the property and the tenant. Good property managers have saved my bacon several times, so consider it money well spent. You won't get calls at 2:00 am when there is a frozen pipe, a fire, a leaky roof, etc. You won't have to chase down rents from late payers or handle any evictions. The manager will take care of all of that. If the property is multi-unit and has several tenants, you'll definitely want to hire a property manager. Otherwise, it's likely you'll have a new full-time job on your hands.

A property with a tenant can be a little trickier to sell. If a buyer wants to use the property right away, they probably won't be interested buying, becoming the new landlord, and waiting for the lease to expire. However, if they like the idea of owning an income-producing property, they may be very inclined to purchase a property that already has a tenant. It's a good idea to speak to an experienced broker who can advise you as to the marketability of the property that comes with a tenant.

There is an upside to accepting a property with a tenant. It comes with regular rental income. That rental income can be used to offset the expenses that come along with the property. If the tenant is reliable, takes good care of the property, and consistently pays rent on time, it could be a real win-win.

No matter what kind of tenant situation you're dealing with, you should always get a copy of the lease(es) and review in detail. You may want to hire outside counsel to review and give you their assessment of potential risks.

Environmental

This is another potentially serious risk. Most properties don't pose significant environmental risks, but some do. For this reason, you'll want to know how the property is used now and how it was used in the past. It's a very good practice to visit the property yourself to see the location, physical condition, and anything that stands out as unsafe or questionable. For instance, large overhead power lines can be problematic. If there is a gas station next door or even a few doors down, that could be an issue. Most underground tanks leak at some point and could very likely infect nearby properties. Look for nearby landfills, industrial areas, auto-repair shops, and anything else that could potentially contaminate the soil or water.

If you do accept a property with environmental contamination, you could be responsible for covering some of the cost of clean-up. Even if your organization never used the property and sold it quickly, you'll still be on the hook for clean-up costs. Everyone in the chain of title after the contamination event will be required to contribute.

If you suspect any potential environmental contamination, you can hire an environmental contractor to perform a *Phase 1* test. If that test shows potential environmental risk, you may consider declining the gift at that point. If the property is highly valuable and you still want to consider accepting it, you can order a *Phase 2* test. Those are much more expensive and include scientific testing. Some charities require the donor to cover these costs. Some cover them on their own.

It's also a great idea to hire a property inspector to perform a thorough inspection. You want to know what you're getting into and what potential environmental problems are lurking. The *Real Estate Questionnaire* at the end of this chapter includes several questions regarding past and present use, as well as potential environmental concerns.

Title

"Clean" title is essential to any gift of real estate. You want to make sure that the donor has the legal ability to transfer the property to your organization without encumbrances. Encumbrances are things such as unpaid taxes, mechanic's liens, deceased persons on the title, etc. Encumbrances can prevent the transfer of title. It is simple to discover if any encumbrances exist on a property. A title company can prepare a "title commitment" on virtually any property. This kind of report gives a description of all the recorded matters concerning title and tells what the title company will insure and what they won't. It is a very smart practice to acquire this report before accepting any gift of real estate and they aren't very expensive.

Even if the encumbrance doesn't prevent transfer of title, it could result in your organization taking on financial responsibility for something unexpected. For example, I worked on a gift of farmland that resulted in over $10,000 in deferred taxes being charged to the charity I worked for. A few years before the gift, the donors entered the property into a "green acres" tax deferral program with the county. As long as the land continued to be actively farmed, the county would defer thousands of dollars in property taxes. Those deferred taxes would ultimately be forgiven if the property was farmed for a certain time period. The green acres program registration should have showed up on the title report, but the attorney we hired to research the title missed it and the donor didn't tell us about it. As soon as the property changed hands and was no longer farmed, the county sent us the very large tax bill. The property hadn't been farmed long enough for the deferred taxes to be forgiven. We asked the donor to contribute cash to help pay the bill, but they were unable to come up with any excess cash to help. Thankfully, the property sold relatively quickly, and we were able to use sales proceeds to cover the tax bill. This is an extreme case and things like this can be avoided if you hire highly experienced professionals to research the title for you. Unfortunately, the attorney we hired was not as experienced as we would have liked.

There is another situation that I've run into several times: deceased persons on the title. Often, when the first spouse passes away, the surviving spouse doesn't retitle their home in just his/her name. Deceased people can't sign deeds, but the fix is simple. The surviving spouse donor can simply retitle the property in her individual name prior to making the donation.

STEP 4: ACCEPT OR DECLINE RESPECTFULLY

Acceptance

If you complete your due diligence process and determine that the gift is acceptable, it's time to move ahead with transferring title. You can either work with your outside counsel or a title company to prepare the transfer documents. If you choose to have a title company prepare the documents, I *highly* recommend having your outside counsel review the documents before moving ahead with the transfer. I've discovered many errors in these documents over the years. It's much less expensive to have it done correctly the first time than try to fix mistakes after the fact. Mistakes in transfer documents can delay or prevent you from selling the property until they're fixed.

Real estate is transferred by deed. There are several different types of deeds. A *Warranty Deed* is probably best, because it means the donor is *warranting* that they have clear title and ability to transfer the property to you. If the property is held in trust, a *Trustee's Deed* can be appropriate. If the donor is only willing to grant a *Quit Claim Deed*, that means they are merely giving up any right they may or may not have in the property. It makes no warrants as to clear title. If you are comfortable with the title report you received, you may be willing to accept a *Quit Claim Deed*. Either way, it is highly advisable to consult with your outside legal counsel as to the manner of deed.

If the gift includes a Life Estate Reserved, the deed must include special language to indicate that the donor is reserving a *Life Estate* for herself. This is a unique kind of transaction, and the average title company doesn't deal with them very often. You'll likely need to explain what's going on in detail so they understand the deed requirements.

Gift Receipts

The donor will need a gift receipt from the charity to claim a charitable income tax deduction for that gift. I am often asked what information should appear on the receipt for a piece of real estate. I think it's a best practice to use the full legal description of the property. Street addresses can be similar to one another, but a legal description is unique. It is the legal language that the municipality uses to identify that specific piece of property. Legal descriptions can be short and simple, or they can be long and complex. You can find the legal description for the property on the most recent deed transferring ownership of that property. You can also likely find it on the qualified appraisal that the donor acquires to substantiate her gift. The language used is often technical and highly specific, so I recommend having a colleague check your work to make sure you've copied the language exactly—word for word.

The charity should *NOT* list the value of the real estate in the gift receipt. It is not the charity's job to assess the value of the property. That is what the *Qualified Appraisal* is for. If someone asks you to include the value of the property in the gift receipt, I advise you to refuse and advise the donor to speak to her tax advisor regarding the appraisal requirement.

The gift receipt should also show the date of the gift. Real estate law differs from state to state and sometimes county to county within the same state, so I advise you to check with your legal counsel to determine the best date to use on your gift receipts. It might be the date the deed is signed and delivered to you. It might be the date the executed deed is recorded with the county. Either way, you'll want to determine which date you will use for gifts of real estate and stick to that procedure. It is a very good practice to send the gift receipt as soon after the gift is made. The donor will need that receipt in time to file her taxes, so time is of the essence. IRS Publication 526 outlines the requirements for gift receipts and the proper timing for sending them to donors.

If you've determined that the property comes with too many risks or you feel you don't have the resources necessary to handle the gift, don't automatically decline. There are other options.

You could work with another charity—such as a community foundation—to accept the real estate, liquidate it, and then pass the proceeds on to you. If so, they will likely retain a small percentage of the sales proceeds to cover their costs. Less than 5% is standard. This can be a real win-win. You get the vast majority of the sales proceeds without having to expend any of your resources or take on any risk.

Alternatively, the community foundation may require the donor to contribute the property to their own Donor Advised Fund before it is liquidated. After liquidation, the donor would have the ability to recommend the proceeds be granted to virtually any public charity they choose—including yours. You may not receive all of the sales proceeds in this case, but it's more than zero. That's what you'd get if you declined.

Another option you may discover is to have the donor contribute the property into *your charity's* fund at a community foundation. They would still handle the liquidation and take on all the risks. After the sale, the proceeds would be available to your organization.

Every organization has its own way of processing gifts on behalf of other charities, so make sure you understand the options clearly before proceeding. It's best to develop a relationship with one of these organizations *prior to* receiving a proposed gift of real estate. You'll be prepared no matter what kind of gift the donor has to offer.

No matter the type of gift, it is very important to communicate your gift acceptance process with the donor.

Let the donor know what you will do with the gift once it's received. It's important to be transparent with donors. If your gift acceptance policies require you to sell immediately and reinvest into a board-approved investment portfolio, make sure you say so. Whatever your intent, let the donor know what will happen to their gift after receipt.

Declining Respectfully

If, after you complete your due diligence, you determine that the gift is unacceptable for whatever reason AND your chosen partner organization is unwilling to accept it— you'll need to decline respectfully.

The donor has offered a generous gift and it is important to acknowledge that. I recommend meeting with the donor to 1) thank them for their offer, and 2) explain *exactly why* you are unable to accept their gift. Explain in clear terms and illustrate your reasons.

I also recommend explaining your decision in writing and giving it to the donor so they can refer back to it later.

If the donor really cares for your organization, they should understand why you must decline. They may decide to consider donating a different asset that brings you less risk.

STEP 5: MANAGE OR LIQUIDATE

Manage

If you accept the gift and determine it is something you wish to keep and use for your charitable mission, that's great! Be sure that you have adequate resources to maintain the property over time. Refer back to the *Marketability + Carrying Costs* section above for a list of expenses you're likely to incur.

The donor may ask you to keep the property rather than sell it. Many charities make the mistake of doing this even though it isn't in their best interests. They keep it to make the donor happy even though they don't need it and it's a bad financial decision. Be honest with your donors and let them know that selling the property will help your organization much more than holding onto the property. Most likely they want you to hold onto it for their own sentimental reasons. They may have inherited the property from a loved one. It may have been the home where they raised their family. If you decide to keep the property, just make sure you're doing it for the right reasons and not simply to satisfy sentimentality. Don't put your organization at risk by keeping it.

Liquidation

Most charities' policies require them to sell all non-cash gifts as soon as possible upon receipt. If you've accepted a piece of real estate, make sure you know your exit plan ahead of time. This goes back to marketability. Hopefully, the property you've accepted is marketable and will sell quickly.

If it's residential property, the most common way to liquidate is with a real estate broker. I recommend interviewing a few brokers ahead of time and selecting a couple to regularly work with. That way, when a donor proposes a gift of real estate, you can consult with your trusted broker(s) and ask their opinion on marketability as part of your due diligence process.

A broker will typically charge a percentage of the sales proceeds as their commission. That is standard and to be expected.

If it's farmland, you may want to consider an auction. This is the standard practice in many rural communities. Ask your donor how farm property is usually liquidated in their area. If auction is common, ask the donor to recommend a couple auction companies for you to interview. Auctioneers commonly charge a *buyer's premium* as their commission. In this case, the buyer pays the commission on top of the sales price. That can be very beneficial to you as the seller.

In some cases, the donor will come to you with a list of interested buyers. That can be a good thing—as long as there is no prearranged sale in the works. I've worked on gifts like this, and they've all gone well. For example, in one case the donor was contributing farmland. Over the years, several neighboring farmers had expressed interest in purchasing the land if they ever decided to sell. The donors provided a list of names and contact information for the interested buyers and the charity sent them an *offer to sell*. The highest bidder won the right to purchase, and we proceeded to closing. If you decide to go this route, you may be missing out on a higher sales price. By opening up the sale to a larger potential market, you may get a higher priced offer. Conversely, if you open up the sale to the larger market by working with a broker, you'll have to pay a sales commission. It's best to carefully weigh your options and choose the one you feel is in the best interest of your organization.

If the real estate is sold within 3 years of the gift, the charity must file IRS Form 8282 with the IRS. This form lets the IRS know how much the real estate was sold for. The IRS matches the 8282 with the 8283 filed by the donor to compare the deduction the donor took with the ultimate sale price of the gift. If the real estate was sold for substantially less than the deduction value claimed by the donor, it is likely the donor could face an audit of that gift. That is one reason the charity should try to get the highest and best value when selling the real estate. **They should not feel compelled to sell to anyone for a discounted price or at unreasonably favorable terms.** An audit by the IRS could view this as "private benefit" on the part of the charity. *Private benefit* can come with stiff financial penalties (25% excise tax, for example), the donor, the charity, employees, and board members of the charity who were involved in the transaction. The charity's nonprofit status can also be revoked in serious cases of private benefit.

In the case of a Life Estate Reserved gift, the charity will receive title at the time of the gift but not the *possessory rights*. This means the charity *owns* it, but the life estate owner has the right to *use* the property. When that person passes away, the charity takes possession by recording the deed and a certified copy of the death certificate with the county. After that, you'll be free to keep or liquidate the property.

SPECIAL CONSIDERATIONS FOR GIFTS OF REAL ESTATE TO FUND CHARITABLE GIFT ANNUITIES OR CHARITABLE REMAINDER TRUSTS

Charitable Gift Annuities:

Accepting a gift of real estate in exchange for a Charitable Gift Annuity (CGA) can be a risky business. When a charity enters into a CGA agreement with a donor, it is agreeing to make fixed payments to the annuitant(s) for life. The payment obligation is a general debt obligation of the charity. As long as the charity has assets, the payments must be made. If the charity accepts a piece of real estate to fund an immediate CGA and the property takes some time to sell, the charity must dip into its own reserves to make those payments. The property may not sell for months or even years. If that happens, the charity could be dipping into its reserves for a long time in order to make the payments. Furthermore, gift annuity payments are based upon the value of the property when it is donated, regardless of how much it sells for. If it sells for less than the value at the time of the gift, the charity will still have to make payments based on that higher amount.

Here's an example:

Real Estate value at time of gift: $350,000
ACGA immediate CGA rate for the income beneficiary: 6%
Annual Payments: $350,000 x 6% = **$21,000**

Net Real Estate Sales Proceeds: $300,000
$300,000 x 6% = $18,000
Charity makes up difference of $3,000/year

If the donor lives another 20 years, that's a difference of **$60,000 the charity must cover from their own reserves.**

It is possible to accept real estate in exchange for a CGA, but you should be aware of the risks when you are creating your policies.

Some charities attempt to mitigate these risks by offering a rate slightly lower than the standard ACGA[21] rate. Additionally, some only issue *deferred* gift annuity agreements in exchange for real estate. That allows the charity time to sell the property before they have to begin making payments.

You'll have to decide for yourself whether you're willing to accept real estate to fund a gift annuity. If you ultimately decide it is too risky, you could seek out another provider who is willing to issue the gift annuity and then pass the majority of the residuum to your organization at the end of the CGA term.

It's best to explore all options ahead of time so that you are prepared when someone inquires about donating real estate in exchange for a CGA. You don't want to have to figure out your options in the moment. Create your own policies and partner with another provider to facilitate gifts that carry more risk than you are comfortable carrying yourself.

Another option is to talk to the donor about using the real estate to fund a Charitable Remainder Trust instead. That solution takes virtually all the risk off the charity. They aren't on the hook to make payments, invest the sales proceeds, or perform administration. The trustee of the CRT is responsible for all of that.

The main concerns from the charity's perspective are:

---

[21] American Council on Gift Annuities, *acga-web.org*

1. The donor can retain the ability to change the charitable beneficiaries in the CRT agreement; and
2. The donor may likely name more than one charitable beneficiary and that could lessen your ultimate share of the gift. These aren't significant risks and are significantly offset by eliminating all the risks associated with accepting real estate to fund a CGA yourself.

Charitable Remainder Unitrust

Appreciated real estate can be a fantastic asset to donate to a CRT. The donor receives a charitable income tax deduction based on the appraised value at the time of the gift. The CRT trustee sells the property tax-free—leaving 100% of the net sales proceeds available to reinvest and make the trust payments to the trust beneficiary(ies). When the CRT comes to its scheduled end, the remaining assets are distributed to the charities the donor named in the trust agreement.

The charitable deduction is not equal to the appraised value of the property; rather, it is *based* upon that value. A simple way to explain the deduction is: "what you're giving minus what you're getting back". Another way to describe it is the "expected remainder of the original gift left over for charity at the end of the trust term". Thankfully, there are several easy-to-use software programs that will calculate the deduction for us very quickly. *PG Calc* and *Crescendo* are the most commonly used software programs.

It is a best practice to utilize the *Flip Charitable Remainder Unitrust* for gifts of real estate. The *Flip* feature gives the trustee time to market and sell the property before making payments to the income beneficiaries. The *Unitrust* feature protects the trust from erosion due to potential volatility in the sales price of the property and fluctuation in the value of trust investments over time. The payments from a *Unitrust* are based on the value of the trust assets each year. For example, if the *Unitrust* payment percentage is 6% and the trust asset value in year one is $100,000, the payment in that year would be $6,000.

$100,000 x 6% = $6,000

If the trust asset value is $110,000 in year two, the payment that year would be $6,600.

$110,000 x 6% = $6,600

Notice the payout percentage does not change. That is constant and is written into the trust document. The payments will fluctuate every year depending on how the trust assets have grown or decreased. This provides some protection for the remainder value to charity.

A Charitable Remainder Annuity Trust (CRAT) is not recommended for gifts of illiquid assets, such as real estate. If it were used, the payout amount would be based on the payout percentage listed in the trust agreement and the value of the gift on the date of the gift. If the property sells for less than the gift value and the investments perform poorly, the trust could be significantly depleted, leaving little to nothing for charity at the end. Furthermore, the *Flip* feature cannot be added to a CRAT. Without that feature, the trustee would have to make payments to the income beneficiaries immediately, regardless of whether the property had sold or not. If the property hasn't sold and the trust has no liquid assets, the only way to make a payment would be to deed shares of the property to the income recipient. That creates a whole host of problems that we won't go into here, but I think you'll agree that isn't something anyone wants. Just know that when dealing with gifts of real estate, the *FLIP CRUT* is the trust type of choice.

Mortgaged Property in a CRT

If a donor contributes a mortgaged property to a Charitable Remainder Trust, it's very likely that it will no longer qualify as a CRT and lose all the tax-exempt benefits that come along with that status.[22] Most debt-encumbered property is not permitted inside a CRT. Furthermore, the gift would still be subject to the Bargain Sale rules discussed above AND could subject the trust a 100% excise tax on debt-financed income when the property is sold.

If the mortgage cannot be removed from the property prior to the gift being made to the CRT, the donor should probably consider donating a different asset.

One risk of note is when charities serve as the *trustee* of a Charitable Remainder Trust. Some charities do this as a matter of practice, but you should be aware of the risks. A trustee is responsible for many things, including:

- Asset management and investment
- Annual tax filings
- Payments to human income beneficiaries
- Protecting assets for the human and charitable beneficiaries

Litigation is not uncommon. The human or charitable beneficiaries may feel the trustee has mismanaged the assets or misreported data on the tax filings and could file a lawsuit. Furthermore, these are *tax-exempt* trusts. The IRS keeps a very close eye on them.

A trustee is considered a *fiduciary*. Fiduciaries have a *legal* duty to protect the interests of those they are charged with protecting. In this case, it's the human and charitable beneficiaries. Violation of that duty could result in severe penalties for the trustee as an organization or for the individual at the organization who is in charge of managing the trust.

---

[22] PLR 9015049

Think twice before agreeing to serve as trustee of a Charitable Remainder Trust. Understand all the risks and get professional legal guidance before you do it.

Sample Real Estate Gift Procedures

1. Conduct initial conversations with donor about gift basics.

2. Donor completes and returns the *Real Estate Questionnaire.*

3. Review completed *Real Estate Questionnaire* and accompanying documentation. If documentation is missing, be sure to acquire it from donor.

4. If any red flags arise from review of *Real Estate Questionnaire*, discuss with donor and resolve—if possible.

5. If no red flags exist, begin the asset transfer.

6. Discuss with donor the method of sale. Get their input, since they know the property better than anyone else. Get recommendation of broker from donor, unless charity wishes to use their own trusted broker.

7. Order title commitment from a title company. If red flags arise on the commitment, work with donor to resolve, if possible.

8. Arrange for property inspection and charity staff visit of the property. If possible, do them simultaneously so staff member can speak with inspector on site. If any red flags result from inspection, work with donor to resolve—if possible.

9. Order closing documents from title company. Warranty deed is best, but donor may not be willing to give a warranty deed. Quit Claim Deed may be acceptable as a second choice.
   a. Title company will need detailed legal information about charity, such as name, Tax ID, address, etc.
   b. Review the documents they prepare with a close eye before sending to donor for signature. Mistakes are common.

10. Send closing documents to donor for signature or deliver in person. A notary will be necessary at signing.

11. Send signed documents to title company. Hand-delivery or trackable overnight delivery is best.

12. Title company records documents.

13. Begin sale process.

14. Work with a real estate broker or auctioneer to liquidate property. Enter into brokerage agreement.

15. Entertain offers as they are received. It is a best practice to review all offers with the donor to get their input. They should be made aware they cannot be the deciding voice, but you appreciate their helpful input.

16. When offer is accepted, work with title company to draft closing documents for sale.
    a. Make sure documents are correct before signing. Mistakes are common.
    b. Inform title company of payment instructions—certified check or money wire?

17. Sales proceeds transfer to charity.

18. Send donor a written acknowledgment of the gift.

Sample **Life Estate Reserved Gift Procedures**

1. Conduct initial conversations about gift basics and review LER illustration from planned giving software.

2. Donor completes and returns the *Real Estate Questionnaire.*

3. Review completed *Real Estate Questionnaire* and accompanying documentation. If documentation is missing, be sure to acquire it from donor.

4. If any red flags arise from review of *Real Estate Questionnaire,* discuss with donor and resolve—if possible.

5. Order title report from a reputable title company. If red flags arise, work with donor to resolve, if possible.

6. Arrange for property inspection and staff visit of the property. If possible, do them simultaneously so staff member can speak with inspector on site. If any red flags result from inspection, work with donor to resolve—if possible.

7. If no red flags exist, begin the asset transfer.

8. Order deed containing LER language from title company.
   a. Title company will need detailed legal information about charity, such as name, Tax ID, address, etc.
   b. Review the documents they prepare with a close eye before sending to donor for signature. Mistakes are common.

9. Send deed and LER Agreement to donor for signature or deliver in person. A notary will be necessary at signing.

10. Send signed documents to title company. Hand-delivery or trackable overnight delivery is best.

11. Title company records documents.

12. Send donor written acknowledgment of the gift. You may consider sending a tax calculation from planned giving software for their deduction.

13. When donor passes away, charity takes possession of the property by recording a copy of the deed and a *certified* copy of the death certificate in the county where they property sits.

14. Begin sale process.

15. Work with broker or auctioneer to liquidate property. Enter into brokerage agreement.

16. Entertain offers as they are received.

17. When offer is accepted, work with title company to draft closing documents.
    a. Make sure documents are correct before signing. Mistakes are common.
    b. Inform title company of payment instructions—certified check or money wire?

18. Sales proceeds transfer to charity.

Sample Real Estate Gift Questionnaire

Please answer the following questions to the best of your ability. Accuracy and thoroughness are vital to the proper care of your gift.

1. Property Address

_____

_____

_____

2. Property Type

_____ Farm Land   (_____ acres)

_____ Raw Land   (_____ acres)

_____ Single-Family Dwelling

_____ Multi-Family Dwelling   (_____ units)

_____ Condominium

_____ Apartment Building   (_____ units)

_____ Industrial Current Use: _____

_____ Warehouse Current Use: _____

_____ Recreational/Vacation Property Current Use: _____

_____ Commercial Property Current Use: _____

_____ Other:_____

3. Is the property currently occupied by a tenant?

_____ No

_____ Yes (please attach a copy of the current lease)

4. If a rental property, is it subject to Section 8 housing?

_____ No

_____ Yes

5. How did you acquire title to the property?

_____ purchase

_____ inheritance

_____ gift

_____ other (please describe) _____

6. When did you acquire property?_____

7. Approximate value at time of your acquisition? _____

8. How is the property titled?

_____ Married couple as joint tenants

_____ Married couple tenants in common

_____ Individual

_____ Individuals as tenants in common

_____ Individuals as joint tenants

_____ Partnership

_____ LLC

_____ Trustee (type of trust): _____

_____ C Corp

_____ S Corp

9. Property Tax Data:

ID Number: _____

Current Tax-Assessed Value: _____

(*Please include a copy of the most recent property tax statement.*)

10. What is the current estimated market value of the property?

_____

11. Have you ever had the property appraised

_____ No

_____ Yes (appraisal date _____ appraised value_____)

12. Legal Description (*Please attach a copy. A deed is the best source.*)

13. Property Insurance (*Please attach a copy of most recent statement.*)

14. Is the property enrolled in any special tax incentive programs?

_____ No

_____ Yes (please describe)

_____

_____

_____

15. Is the property located in a registered historic district or subject to any preservation restrictions, such as easements?

_____ No

_____ Yes (please describe)

_____

_____

_____

16. How is the property currently zoned?

_____

17. Is the property currently subject to a mortgage?

_____ No

_____ Yes

Current balance: _____

18. Have you depreciated the property on your taxes?

_____ No

_____ Yes (*We may request copies of your depreciation schedule and list of improvements.*)

19. Do you have any of the following documents? (*Please attach copies.*)

_____ Title insurance policy

_____ Abstract of title

_____ Survey

_____ Registered property abstract

_____ Certificate of title

_____ Environmental test reports

20. Is the property adjacent to any lake, river, drainage ditch or other waterway?

_____ No

_____ Yes (please describe)

_____

_____

_____

22. Are there any equipment, furnishings, or other personal property are included with the property?

_____ No

_____ Yes (please describe)

_____

_____

_____

23. Does the property have access to a public road?

_____ No

_____ Yes

24. What have been the past uses of the property since you acquired it?

_____

_____

_____

26. Is any part of the property or adjacent property being used or to the best of your knowledge ever been used for any of the following?

Industrial or manufacturing	Yes	No	Unknown
Fueling station	Yes	No	Unknown
Motor repair	Yes	No	Unknown
Commercial printing	Yes	No	Unknown
Dry cleaning	Yes	No	Unknown
Photo developing lab	Yes	No	Unknown
Dump, junkyard, storage, disposal, processing or recycling?			
	Yes	No	Unknown
Cleaning or janitorial service	Yes	No	Unknown
Chemical plant	Yes	No	Unknown
Methamphetamine lab	Yes	No	Unknown
Paint store or factory	Yes	No	Unknown
Wood stripping or refinishing shop			
	Yes	No	Unknown
Fiberglass manufacturing or distributing			
	Yes	No	Unknown
Tannery	Yes	No	Unknown
Mine or quarry	Yes	No	Unknown

27. Are there now or have there every been any of the following on or buried beneath the property?

Septic systems	Yes	No	Unknown
Wells	Yes	No	Unknown

Buried waste materials   Yes   No   Unknown

Abandoned cars, trucks, or other vehicles or tires or parts

                                Yes   No   Unknown

Batteries   Yes   No   Unknown

Barrels or containers of pesticides, herbicides, fertilizers, paint, or other chemicals

stored or buried   Yes   No   Unknown

Industrial drums (55 gallons or greater) stored on the property

                                Yes   No   Unknown

Fill dirt from a contaminated site or from an unknown origin

                                Yes   No   Unknown

Pits, ponds, or lagoons having to do with waste treatment or waste disposal

                                Yes   No   Unknown

Areas of stained soil on the property

                                Yes   No   Unknown

Above or underground storage tanks

                                Yes   No   Unknown

Vent pipes or fill pipes protruding from the ground or next to the structure

                                Yes   No   Unknown

Flooring, drains, or walls located within a building that are stained by substances

other than water or that give off a foul odor

                                Yes   No   Unknown

Transformer, capacitor or any hydraulic equipment containing PCBs

                                Yes   No   Unknown

Floor tiles, ceiling material, insulation or other building materials containing

asbestos   Yes   No   Unknown

28. Do you know of any environmental assessments or inspections of the property that indicated the presence of hazardous substances, asbestos, PCBs or petroleum products on or contamination?

_____ No

_____ Yes (please describe)

_____

_____

_____

29. Do you know of any past or present governmental notifications or environmental liens relating to past or recurrent violations of environmental laws?

_____ No

_____ Yes (please describe)

_____

_____

_____

30. Do you know of any past, threatened, or pending lawsuits or administrative proceedings concerning a release or threatened release of any hazardous substance or petroleum product involving the property?

_____ No

_____ Yes (please describe)

_____

_____

_____

32. Has there ever been a pest infestation, including but not limited to insects and/or rodents?

_____ No

_____ Yes (please describe)

_____

I understand that the truth and accuracy of my answers to the previous questions will be relied upon when evaluating my proposed gift of real estate. I certify that each of the answers is true, accurate, and complete to the best of my knowledge.

_____

Signature   Date

_____

Print name

If the person signing is not the party using and occupying the property, please list:

Name of current user _____

Phone number _____

Mailing address

_____

_____

_____

Chapter 5:
Gifts of Life Insurance

Gifts of Life Insurance can strike fear in the heart of even the most stalwart Gift Planner. It's a complex asset and can seem intimidating, but with a few key pieces of knowledge, you can master it.

Let's take the fear out of Life Insurance by putting it through our 5-Step process.

1. **Know the Basics**
2. **Ask for the Right Information**
3. **Evaluate for Opportunity and Risk**
4. **Accept or Decline Respectfully**
5. **Manage or Liquidate**

STEP 1: KNOW THE BASICS OF LIFE INSURANCE

Types of Life Insurance

Life Insurance comes in two basic types: "***term***" and "***permanent***".

Term is like your car insurance. You pay premiums to cover financial loss. If you continue to pay your premiums, the insurance is there to protect you. If/when you stop paying premiums, the policy is canceled. The premiums you pay are solely to cover the cost of insurance. Term life insurance expires after a certain period of time—1 year, 10 years, 20 years, etc. You can purchase insurance for the amount of time you need it. If you want to renew it, at the end of the term you reapply.

Permanent insurance provides protection from financial losses, but it also includes an additional component. That additional component is kind of like a savings account. The premiums you pay cover the cost of insurance AND some of the premium is set aside to be invested. As long as you continue to pay premiums, the insurance remains in effect. Permanent insurance doesn't expire like term insurance does. At some point in the future, the invested portion could be available for you to withdraw. **It's called the "cash value".**

In both cases, if the insured person dies with the insurance in place, the **Death Benefit** is paid to the beneficiaries of the policy. The death benefit or "face value" is a set amount and generally doesn't change once the policy is put into place.

You may run across policies that are a *blend* of term and permanent. The premiums tend to be lower than that of permanent insurance but higher than term. The ratio of term to permanent varies from contract to contract. These policies accumulate some cash value, but it's not as much as a permanent policy.

Why would someone want a *blended* policy? In my experience, it's because the premiums are relatively low compared to the death benefit. We will talk more about this kind of insurance policy later in Step 3 when we address opportunity and risk.

Ways to Give | Tax Deductions | Appraisals

There are two basic ways to give life insurance to charity. **First, a donor can name a charity/charities as full or partial beneficiary of the policy.** When the insured person passes away, the death benefit is paid out to the beneficiaries. A donor can name both family and charity as beneficiaries of the same policy. She continues to own and control the policy, so she can change her mind and alter those beneficiaries as long as she owns the contract. **No income tax charitable deduction is available because the donor continues to own and control the policy. Upon her death, the death benefit going to charity may be claimed as an estate tax charitable deduction.**

Second, a donor can donate the actual policy to charity. Old or new policies can be donated. If a donor has a policy she no longer needs, she can donate it. If she likes the idea of giving insurance as a charitable gift, she may purchase a new policy and donate it to charity. In either case, there may be ongoing premiums required. **If the donor continues to pay those premiums after the policy is donated, they may be claimed as an income tax charitable deduction.**

The basic premise behind donating an insurance policy is that the donor makes regular premium payments over time and at the end of her lifetime, the death benefit is much larger than the sum of all the premiums paid. This can work well if the math pans out. If the donor lives a very long time, they could end up paying more in premiums than the death benefit is worth. **It's best if the policy doesn't require the donor to make premium payments for her entire life, but rather requires premiums only for a set number of years.** I've seen several cases where the donor goes into a care facility and is no longer able to pay the ongoing premiums. The policy must be canceled, and the charity gets little to nothing compared to the death benefit the donor intended to give.

Permanent Life Insurance is typically the kind that people donate to charity. Term can be donated, but the charity only receives a payout if the donor passes away before the term ends. In either case, the donor may be entitled to charitable income tax deductions for the *cash value* of the contract when donated AND any ongoing premiums paid after the contract is donated. There is no estate tax charitable deduction available as there is in the case of a gift of life insurance by beneficiary designation.

If ongoing premiums are required, the donor may pay the premiums directly to the insurance company OR make a donation to the charity in the amount of the premium and let them pay it. The second option may be a good idea in some cases. Premiums paid directly to the insurance company are considered gifts *"for the use of the charity"*. Those kinds of gifts come with a lower deductibility limit (20% of *Adjusted Gross Income*) and any unused portion of the deduction cannot be carried forward to future tax years. If the donor makes a contribution directly *to the charity* and *the charity* pays the premium, the donor has made a *direct gift to charity*. A direct cash gift comes with a 60% AGI deductibility limit.[23] Any unused portion of the deduction may be carried forward up to 5 additional tax years.

If you want to get fun and creative, the donor could donate appreciated stock to the charity, let them liquidate it and use the proceeds to pay the premium. That can be of great benefit to the donor since they could bypass the capital gains on the appreciation AND be entitled to a fair market value deduction for the gift. Gifts of stock come with a 30% AGI deductibility limit plus the 5-year carry-forward. *You can read about the special benefits of donating appreciated stock in Chapter 2.*

When an existing policy is donated, it may have some "cash value" built up inside it. That may entitle the donor to an additional charitable deduction. If the cash value is in excess of $5,000, the policy must be appraised to determine the deductible amount. The calculation to determine the deduction is lengthy, but the simple way I explain it is *"the lesser of cost basis or cash value"*. Remember, cost basis is generally what you paid for something (in this case accumulated premiums). The technical term for the appraised value of a life insurance contract is *"interpolated terminal reserve"*.

The appraisal must be completed by an independent third party. It can't be the donor and it can't be the insurance company. In the past, I've worked with Charitable Solutions, LLC to appraise charitable gifts of life insurance. They've always done a nice job and the price is reasonable.

The charity will have to sign IRS Form 8283 if the donor wishes to take a charitable income tax deduction, but the charity should NOT complete the form for the donor. Nor should the charity sign before the form is completed and signed by both the donor and the appraiser.

---

[23] 50% AGI limit for tax years after 2025

Insurable Interest

We can't go around purchasing life insurance contracts on anyone we want. First, we must establish that we have an *Insurable Interest* in that person's life. We must prove that when they die, we will suffer a financial loss.

State departments of insurance regulate the sale of life insurance to their residents. They each define *Insurable Interest* in their own way. When it comes to charities owning life insurance on a donor, the rules differ from state to state. You'll want to know the rules for your state before you have conversations with donors and their advisors about accepting a gift of a life insurance policy. Check with your state's department of insurance to find out the details.

In many cases, it's difficult for a charity to prove they have an insurable interest on a donor. If they can't, they won't be able to *purchase* a policy on a donor. They can; however, receive an existing policy from a donor as a gift.

I've been involved in many gift planning conversations where the donor and her advisor have proposed contributing cash to the charity and then asking the charity to use that cash to apply for and purchase insurance on the donor.

Because of insurable interest laws, it's much easier for the donor to apply for the insurance and then once the contract is issued, she donates the policy to charity. That way, the charity doesn't have to prove insurable interest. Virtually anyone can purchase insurance on their own life without having to prove insurable interest. Insurance laws assume we humans have an inherent financial interest in our own longevity.

STEP 2: ASK FOR THE RIGHT INFORMATION

At the end of this chapter, you will find a *Sample Gift of Life Insurance Questionnaire*. This document is meant to help you get started. You will want to edit it to meet your organization's specific needs.

When someone wants to donate an insurance policy, the best way to gather all the necessary information is to request an *in-force illustration*. This illustration is produced by the insurance company issuing the policy. They can be created for existing policies OR new policies that haven't yet been issued.

The *in-force illustration* will list:
- Insured's name(s),
- Premium amount,
- Death benefit,
- Premium schedule (how often and how long payments must be made),
- Ratio of term to permanent insurance (in the case of a *blended* policy),
- Guaranteed rate of return on any cash value, and
- Any outstanding loans.

Reading life insurance illustrations takes some practice and instruction. It took me years to become decent at it and I was reviewing several per year. I recommend working with an experienced life insurance professional who can help you to understand what you're looking at and to evaluate whether it is in your best interest to accept or not. Whomever you choose should understand your needs and limitations.

Potential Concerns Upon Reviewing an In-Force Illustration

- Unusually high illustrated rate of internal return. Illustrating a rate of return that is too high could result in things like increased premiums over time if the contract's underlying investments do not yield as much as illustrated. That's a hard conversation to have with the donor and/or her family when you have to let them know they must increase their premium payment to keep the contract in force.

- Blend of term and permanent life insurance. A contract can combine both types of insurance and is usually done to increase death benefit and lower premium cost. These contracts don't accumulate as much cash value. If the donor reaches a point where she is no longer able to make premium payments, there is limited cash in the contract and that will reduce options to salvage some value from the contract. There may be less cash in the contract than the donor has paid in accumulated premiums. That is a hard conversation to have with the donor and/or her family.

- Outstanding loans on the policy: Life insurance policy holders can sometimes take loans against their policies. If a policy with a loan is donated to charity, the contribution will fall under the *Bargain Sale* rules. The donor will likely have to recognize income in the amount of the outstanding loan.

STEP 3: EVALUATE FOR OPPORTUNITY AND RISK

Now that you have a firm grasp on the basics of donating life insurance to charity and you've reviewed the illustration, you'll be better prepared to evaluate the proposed gift.

Gift Life Insurance by Beneficiary Designation

If a donor names your organization as beneficiary of a life insurance policy, there is virtually nothing you need to do, except steward the donor until they pass away. At that time, you'll likely need to file a death claim form along with a certified copy of the death certificate with the insurance company. This is a pretty risk-free kind of gift that any organization can handle.

I still recommend getting a copy of the *in-force illustration* and performing your usual due diligence so that you know exactly what's being offered.

Occasionally, a donor may ask your organization to pay premiums for a policy on which she has named you a beneficiary. This is illegal and considered "private benefit". Since the donor still owns and controls the policy, you would essentially be giving her money in the form of premium payments. Don't do it.

Gift of Life Insurance by Policy Donation

There are a few risks when accepting a life insurance contract. They come with virtually no financial liability, unless you have agreed to pay the premiums. **Most charities, as a matter of practice, do not pay premiums. It can be a significant drain on the charity's cash flow.** If the donor lives a long time, you could end up paying more in premiums than you receive as the death benefit. You also have to consider the time value of money. When considering inflation, is it a good investment of your charitable dollars today for the potential payoff years later?

The biggest risk you will probably face is the administrative burden of holding a life insurance contract. You have to pay a good deal of attention to the contract. You can't just put it in a drawer and ignore it. It is kind of like a living, breathing thing. It requires maintenance and sometimes that maintenance can be significant. Management details are covered a little later in Step 5.

If you decide you DON'T want to accept gifts of policies, check with your local community foundation to see if they would accept the gift on your behalf and take care of the administration. Some are happy to do this for charities in their community if they are holding your endowment fund. Some may also do it and then charge a service fee when the death benefit is paid out upon the donor's death.

STEP 4: ACCEPT OR DECLINE RESPECTFULLY

If you decide to accept the donation of a policy, great! Life Insurance policies are donated through a process called *Assignment*. The donor completes a form provided by the insurance company indicating that they wish to *assign* ownership to your organization. To do so, they will need some vital data including:
- Charity's Legal Name
- Charity's Federal Tax Identification Number
- Charity's Legal Address

No matter the type of gift, it is very important to communicate your gift acceptance process with the donor.

Let them know what you will do with the gift once it's received. It's important to be transparent with donors. If your gift acceptance policies require you to liquidate an asset immediately and reinvest into a board-approved investment portfolio, make sure you say so. If you'll retain the policy but not pay any ongoing premiums, let them know that. Whatever your intent, let the donor know what will happen to their gift after receipt.

If you decide to decline the gift, it is VERY important to explain exactly WHY. People don't like to hear the word "no". Donors can feel especially offended if they offer a gift and you decline without an explanation. If a donor really cares about your organization, they will understand why you've declined their gift. You need only to take the time to explain. It's a good idea to do this verbally and accompany your conversation with a written explanation. The gift may not be 100% lost. You may want to ask them to consider naming your organization as beneficiary of the contract instead of donating the actual policy. It's always a good idea to suggest other options when you must decline a gift. It can preserve a good working relationship AND secure a valuable gift.

STEP 5: MANAGEMENT AND STEWARDSHIP

If a donor wants to donate an actual policy to your organization, you will have some administrative duties to perform.

1. If accepted, send the donor a gift receipt for the gift of the policy. *It should NOT include any values*—just the basic information such as gift date, policy number, and insurance company. The gift date is usually the date the policy is "assigned" to you. You can find this on the Form 712. This is an IRS form that the insurance company will provide to you at your request. It provides all the essential technical data for the policy.

2. Make sure your organization is named BOTH owner AND beneficiary of the policy. You don't want the death benefit going to one of the donor's heirs by mistake. That would be a gigantic headache.

3. Check with the insurance company to see if the premium notices can be mailed directly to the donor since they are likely going to be the ones making the payments.

4. Send the donor a gift receipt each time they make a premium payment. She will need these receipts in order to claim income tax deductions for the premium payments she makes.

5. Keep an eye on the policy to make sure premiums are being made and the policy is healthy. You may want to work with an experienced insurance professional to help you review policies on an ongoing basis. Determine how often you need to review each contract you accept and design a system to remind you when it's time to request an *in-force illustration* from the insurance company.

6. When the donor passes away, file a claim form and certified death certificate with the insurance company. Proceeds are usually sent to the charity within weeks of filing the claim form and death certificate.

What if you DO accept a policy, and at some point, the donor is no longer willing/able to pay ongoing premiums? If you run into this situation, there are some options.

1. **Charity Pays:** Generally, it's not a great idea for charities to pay these premiums, but you can do it. Premiums can be an expensive drain on your cash flow. It may be a good idea if the donor's life expectancy is short. If it's long, it may not be the best option. I know, it's morbid to think of it in those terms, but death is a primary element of life insurance.

2. **Liquidate the Policy:** Since your organization owns the policy, you can choose to liquidate it, take whatever cash value it has accumulated and put it toward your charitable mission.

3. **Convert to "Reduced Paid-Up":** This will discontinue any ongoing premiums, but the death benefit will likely be reduced. The insurance stays in place and you will still be able to claim the death benefit upon the donor's passing.

4. **Sell the policy:** This is another morbid topic, but you may be able to find a buyer for the contract. There are companies that purchase life insurance contracts. These transactions are commonly referred to as *vatical settlements*. The buyer pays you a set dollar amount. They become the new owner and beneficiary of the contract and are also responsible for any ongoing premiums. Some charities are morally opposed to selling life insurance contracts, but I recommend at least considering this as an option before dismissing it.

It's best to compare all four options side by side and determine which one is in your organization's best interest.

Whatever you decide to do, it's a very good practice to maintain an open conversation with the donor and/or her family to let them know there are options. The worst thing to do is to do nothing and let the insurance lapse. If you do that, the charity gets nothing and all the money the donor has paid in premiums goes to waste.

SPECIAL CONSIDERATIONS FOR GIFTS OF LIFE INSURANCE FOR CHARITABLE GIFT ANNUITIES AND CHARITABLE REMAINDER TRUSTS

Occasionally, a donor or her advisor will propose contributing a life insurance policy to either a Charitable Gift Annuity or Charitable Remainder Trust. Both should be approached with *extreme* caution.

First, let's look at the Charitable Gift Annuity (CGA) situation. If a life insurance policy is used to fund a CGA, where will the charity come up with the money to make the annuity payments? They could cash out the policy and use that cash as the basis for the gift. The insurance contract would need to be appraised to determine the value. **The appraised value is NOT going to be the death benefit.** It will be the *interpolated terminal reserve* value we discussed earlier. If you're comfortable with the risks, I recommend a *deferred* CGA for situations like this. The deferral period allows time for appraisal of the life insurance contract before payments must be made. After all, you can't calculate a CGA payment amount until you know the value of the gift. It's the donor's responsibility to have the contract appraised—not the charity's. However, the charity needs the appraisal value before they can issue the CGA contract. It's a bit of a chicken and egg situation that can make your head spin. In this case, I think it would be appropriate for the charity to arrange for and pay for the appraisal, *BUT* they would need to deduct the cost of the appraisal from the appraised value of the gift when they write the CGA contract.

It would be much simpler if the donor cashed out the policy and donated the cash to fund the CGA. They may have to realize some income tax when they cash out the contract, but hopefully the charitable deduction from the CGA would minimize or completely offset that extra tax.

There is another option, but it is quite risky. The charity could dip into its own cash reserves to make the annuity payments until the insured passes away and the charity receives the death benefit. Let's look at the risks of this option.

The premiums may need to be paid for a long period of time and possibly until the insured dies. If the charity dips into its reserves to make the annuity payments, they could be doing so for a very long time.

Additionally, the donor could stop making premium payments at some point for any variety of reasons. The charity is still obligated to make annuity payments to the annuitant(s) until their death(s). If premium payments aren't made, the contract is likely to lapse—leaving the charity with little to nothing. They could cash out the contract, but that may not cover the cost of the ongoing CGA payments. I think you can see why I recommend to approach this with *extreme* caution.

Next, let's look at a Charitable Remainder Trust (CRT) funded with a life insurance contract.

I've been approached several times about using life insurance as the investment vehicle inside a CRT. In some cases, the donor or her advisor proposed donating an existing life insurance contract to a CRT. In other cases, they suggested donating cash or stock to the CRT and then using those assets to *purchase* a new life insurance contract. Let's review both situations.

First, how would it work if someone donated a life insurance contract to fund a CRT? This isn't a bad idea on its face, but it can pose some significant complications. The trustee could liquidate the policy and use the cash value to invest in a diversified portfolio. It's not much different from donating any type of non-cash asset to a CRT—*as long as the trustee will be liquidating the policy.*

I do not recommend keeping the life insurance contract in place inside the CRT.

First of all, if the only asset in the CRT is a life insurance contract, how will the trustee make the necessary payments to the income beneficiaries? They would have to make cash withdrawals from the policy. Unless the policy has a LOT of cash value built up, repeated cash withdrawals could deplete the contract down to nothing. If that happens, the trust terminates, income beneficiaries receive no more payments, and the charity gets nothing.

Second, the CRT assets must be valued every year in order to file the trust tax return with the IRS. Valuing the policy every single year can be an expensive and time-consuming process.

Lastly, it is never prudent to sink all your assets into one investment. If the only asset inside the CRT is a life insurance contract, the trustee is *putting all the eggs in one basket.* Trustees are bound by a *fiduciary* standard which requires them to act in the best interest of both the income beneficiaries and the charitable beneficiaries. Diversification is the bedrock of prudent investment strategy. Any trustee that doesn't diversify investments is not acting in the best interest of those they are obligated to protect. Some may argue that the cash value in the insurance contract can be invested by the insurance company in a wide variety of assets. Even so, the insurance company is still just one company—no matter how they invest the cash value of the policy. All the eggs are still invested by one company and therefore in *one basket.*

What if the donor wishes to contribute cash, stock, or other assets to the CRT and then have the trustee use those assets to *purchase a new* life insurance contract? In that case, the question of *insurable interest* arises. Does the trustee have an *insurable interest* on the life of the insured? In most cases the answer is *NO.* If by some miracle the answer is yes, I refer you to my earlier comments on investing all or most of the trust's assets in an insurance policy. It probably isn't a wise investment choice.

Sample **Life Insurance Gift Procedures (New or Existing Contract)**

1. Conduct initial conversations with donor about gift basics. Be sure donor understands who will be paying any ongoing premiums.

2. Provide donor with the *Life Insurance Gift Questionnaire* to complete and return to you along with an "in-force illustration". They will need to request the illustration from the insurance company.

3. Review *Life Insurance Gift Questionnaire* and "in-force illustration".

4. If *Questionnaire* and illustration raise no red flags, begin asset transfer. Donor works with insurance company to assign ownership of existing contract to charity. They will likely need the following information:

   a. Charity's Federal Tax ID Number
   b. Charity's Address
   c. Charity's Legal Name

5. Many states do not allow for the charity to apply for life insurance on a donor or prospective donor unless they can prove they have an "insurable interest" in that person's life. *It is a best practice for the donor to apply for the insurance and then assign ownership to charity once issued.*

6. Donor will need to acquire and pay for a qualified appraisal to take an income tax charitable deduction for any cash value inside the contract.

7. Find out where the insurance company will send premium notices. If the donor is paying the premium, try to arrange for notices to be sent to the donor. If that isn't possible, you will need to send notices to the donor as soon as received. If charity is paying the premiums, they'll want to receive notices directly.

8. Send the donor a written acknowledgment for the gift of the insurance policy *and* for all future premium payments paid by donor.

9. Send donor a gift receipt every time they make a premium payment. If donor wishes to pay premiums with stock, they can transfer stock to charity to be liquidated and then charity uses sales proceeds to pay the premium. This is a separate gift and will require a gift receipt for the gift of stock, but not the premium payment.

10. Put the policy on a schedule to be reviewed every 1-3 years. Different contracts may be put on different review schedules, depending on their individual details.

11. When the insured passes away, file claim form with insurance company. They will likely require a Certified copy of the Death Certificate and completed claim form.

Sample Life Insurance Gift Questionnaire

1. Would you like to donate a new or existing contract? NEW   EXISTING

2. What is the death benefit amount? _____

3. Who is the insurance carrier? _____

4. Are ongoing premiums required? YES   NO
    a. If Yes, how often are premiums due and what is the payment amount?
    _____

5. Who is the insured? _____

6. What is their relationship to you? _____

7. *Please request an "in-force illustration" of the policy from the insurance carrier and return with this questionnaire. The illustration will contain very important information about the contract.*

Chapter 6:
Gifts of Agricultural Assets

I f you live or work in an agricultural area, it may come as no surprise that farmers donate things like *harvested crops*, *livestock*, and *farm machinery* to charity. It makes sense if you think about it. It's what farmers have and they're valuable assets that charities can sell.

Each of these three asset types requires specialized care when donated to charity, but once you know what to do, it's pretty simple. When handled properly, these kinds of gifts can work out great for both the farmer and the charity.

Harvested crops, livestock, and machinery offer BIG opportunity for charities. The assets are valuable and easy to liquidate. They are typically much larger gifts than a farmer could make in cash. Most of the time, they are a much more tax-efficient gift for the farmer than cash. If your donor base includes farmers, you'll want to get your "farm asset" gift program up and running sooner than later. Once you've used the resources in this chapter to get your infrastructure in place, start letting farmers know that they can donate crops, livestock, and machinery AND that you're happy to accept them.

Let's apply our 5-Step Process so you'll be prepared for gifts of crops, livestock, and farm machinery. We'll look at each type individually within each of the five steps so you clearly understand the special nuances of each one.

      1. **Know the Basics**
      2. **Ask for the Right Information**
      3. **Evaluate for Opportunity and Risk**
      4. **Accept or Decline Respectfully**
      5. **Manage or Liquidate**

At the end of this chapter, you'll find *Sample* procedures and questionnaires for each type of asset. These documents are meant to help you get started. You'll definitely want to edit them according to your organization's specific needs.

STEP 1: KNOW THE BASICS

Harvested Crops

The most common types of crops you'll probably run into are corn, wheat, and soybeans. After the crops have been harvested, farmers will transport them to the local grain elevator to sell. In the case of a charitable gift of crops—the farmer will deliver to the elevator in the name of a favorite charity. The charity contacts the elevator and requests them to be sold and the proceeds sent to the charity. It's that simple.

If the farmer sells the crops herself, the proceeds are subject to ordinary income tax and self-employment taxes. There is often little to no basis in the crops; therefore, the entire sales price is subject to taxes. Needless to say, crops are highly taxable assets, which is one reason farmers will choose them as the best asset to donate.

Farmers deliver the crops to the elevator in the name of the charity. The charity sells the crops, and the farmer does not recognize the income on the sale. The charitable deduction for ordinary income property such as crops is the *lesser of cost basis or fair market value*. The crops have little to no basis, so the farmer is not likely to receive any income tax charitable deduction for the gift. The gift does help them to avoid tax on income they may not need *AND* make a sizable charitable gift. It's much more efficient than selling, recognizing the income, making a gift of cash, and taking a charitable deduction for the cash gift. In most cases, the charitable deduction for the cash gift won't offset all of the income and subsequent tax the way a gift of crops does.

Gifts of crops tend to come seasonally—at harvest time. Depending on the growing zone, that's usually in the late summer or early fall.

Livestock

Farm animals, such as beef cattle and hogs, are the most common livestock gifts you'll probably see. They are liquidated in much the same way as crops. Farmers transport them to a sale barn where they are sold by auction. In the case of charitable contribution, the farmer will deliver the livestock in the name of the charity. The charity works with the sale barn to auction the livestock and send proceeds to the charity. It's a pretty straightforward process.

When a farmer sells livestock, the proceeds are subject to ordinary income tax and self-employment taxes. Just like crops, livestock are highly taxed assets. You can see why a farmer might choose this as a good asset to give.

Some types of livestock are considered capital gain property and thus subject to lower capital gains tax rates. That only applies to animals used for "draft", "dairy breeding", or "sports". So, unless your donor has animals that fall into these categories, their livestock is probably going to be considered ordinary income property.

The charitable deduction for ordinary income property is the *lesser of cost basis or fair market value*. Livestock tends to have little to no basis; therefore, the farmer is likely to receive no charitable income tax deduction for the gift. The gift does help them to avoid income and self-employment tax when sold, so it can be a very tax-efficient asset to donate. It's much more efficient than selling, recognizing the taxes, and then making a cash gift to charity. The charitable deduction for the cash gift probably won't offset all the income associated with the sale anyway. The gift of the livestock will.

Farm Machinery

Big machines, like tractors and harvesters, cost a fortune. The newer models are extremely technologically advanced and can even be programmed to drive themselves. When farmers are ready to upgrade to a newer model, they will most often sell the older machine at a machine auction. Machine auctions tend to happen in Spring and Fall when the machines are not needed for farm activity. Farm machinery is considered an ordinary income asset and subject to ordinary income tax rates, which are some of the highest rates a taxpayer will pay.

While the farmer uses the machinery, she is likely to *depreciate* the value on her taxes. Depreciation provides a tax deduction for the decrease in the machine's value over time. Depreciation also reduces the farmer's "basis" in the asset. (Remember, basis is the amount you have invested in an asset.) When you sell, your taxable income is based on the difference between the sales price and your basis. If your basis has been reduced by depreciation, most or all of the sale price is going to be taxable and at those higher ordinary income rates. Machinery is not likely to be subject to self-employment taxes, but the sales prices are often very high and therefore come with a hefty income tax bill.

Farmers can donate their farm machinery to charity. They simply transfer the title to a favorite charity. The charity will often work with a machinery auctioneer to liquidate the machinery for them. That way, they are likely to get the highest sales price possible and the auctioneer takes care of just about everything to do with the sales process. Nice and easy for the charity.

Because the charity is selling the machinery, the farmer doesn't recognize the income tax on the sale. The charitable deduction for ordinary income property is the *lesser of cost basis or fair market value*. If the farmer's basis in the machine is low or zero, the resulting charitable deduction will thus be low or zero as well. The gift does allow the farmer to avoid the extra income on the sale, which is almost always more tax-efficient than selling, recognizing the income, and then making a cash gift to charity. The cash gift probably won't offset all the income from the sale the way an outright gift of machinery does.

Machine auctions can be really fun. Many farmers attend as a social activity—even if they aren't bidding or selling. There might be food vendors and other activities happening. You might want to attend for the fun of it and to get a little publicity for your organization. It certainly can't hurt to spread the word to those you meet that someone donated a piece of machinery and you'll be selling it to further your mission. It just might inspire another farmer to do the same thing.

STEP 2: ASK FOR THE RIGHT INFORMATION

Crops, Livestock, and Machinery are pretty easy to liquidate and don't come with a great deal of risk. (We'll look at risks more carefully in Step 3.) As a result, there isn't much information you'll need to gather on the front end.

At the end of this chapter, you'll find sample questionnaires for livestock, and machinery. They are designed to help you collect important information about the assets prior to accepting them. I've not included one for crops or livestock because they would be about two questions long. Many times the donor just drops crops at the elevator before you've even had a conversation about the gift.

You may want to include instructions and a sample Deed of Gift for gifts of harvested crops on your website to make sure the gift is made properly—even if the donor doesn't consult with you first.

For harvested crops, you'll want to know the estimated value of the gift to make sure it meets your gift minimums. Many charities set low or no gift minimum when it comes to crops because they are so simple to receive and liquidate, and they bring virtually no risk. You'll want the farmer to alert you that the gift is coming and let you know *immediately* when the crops have been delivered to the grain elevator in your organization's name. You don't want them sitting there unsold for a period of time. You'll want to have the elevator sell them right away to avoid the fluctuation in crop prices. Prices can go up and down quite a bit over short periods of time.

Livestock is a little bit more complex because it requires a bit more coordination. You will want to know the type of animals you'll be receiving. You'll want to know the estimated value to make sure it meets your gift minimums. Sometimes, someone from a sale barn will visit a farm to provide an estimated sale price before the animals are delivered to them. You will want to know when the sale barn conducts auctions. They are usually done on specific days of the week and it's a good idea to reduce the amount of time between delivery and auction because during that time the animals will need to be fed and cared for. That costs money and will reduce your ultimate sale price.

Machinery is probably the most valuable agricultural asset you can receive, but it is still pretty simple to accept and process. You'll want to know the estimated sale price to make sure it meets with your gift minimum. An auctioneer may be willing to give you a ballpark estimate. You'll probably want to ask the donor for an auctioneer recommendation. They are likely going to have a preference as to which one they would use.

STEP 3: EVALUATE FOR OPPORTUNITY AND RISK

Agricultural assets bring relatively low risk to a charity, but you should know about the risks so you can prepare accordingly.

The primary risk from a gift of **harvested crops** is the timing of the sale. Prices can fluctuate quite a bit over a short period of time. To mitigate this, be sure to communicate to your donors that they should notify you *immediately* when crops have been delivered in your name to a grain elevator. That way, you can have the crops sold right away and potentially avoid wide fluctuations in price.

Livestock can be a simple gift, but you need to remember that these are living things and require food, housing, and medical care. If you can time the gift close to the date of a livestock auction, you can reduce these potential costs. You may want to ask the sale barn what kind of insurance they carry to cover risks to the animals while in their care and whether that insurance might cover your losses as well.

Livestock does bring a unique public relations risk. Not everyone is comfortable with the thought of accepting a gift of living creatures and selling them to be slaughtered for food or other products. If this is contrary to your organization's charitable mission or values, you may want to decline livestock gifts and write that into your gift acceptance policies. I recommend including an explanation in your gift acceptance policies. People like to know *why* you won't accept a certain gift. Even if the selling of animals for food doesn't go against your organization's mission or values, a certain portion of your donor base and/or staff may find it distasteful or offensive. You'll have to weigh that when considering whether to accept livestock gifts as a matter of principle.

Farm machinery is a relatively risk-free type of gift. There is the possibility that the machine could be damaged or even stolen while on the auctioneer's lot. I recommend asking the auctioneer what kind of insurance they carry that might cover losses due to damage or theft while in their care. If they carry none or only a little insurance, you may want to insure the machinery yourself. The insurance shouldn't be very expensive since you probably won't own the machine for long. It may only be days or weeks between the time of the gift and the time of sale.

For all three asset types, you'll want to make sure the donor has not entered into any sale agreements (written or oral) with a buyer, grain elevator, sale barn, etc. If they have, the donor could be in violation of that agreement by donating the asset to charity. Furthermore, if the charity ultimately sells to that buyer, elevator, sale barn, etc., the transaction could be ruled a "prearranged sale" by the IRS and the donor may have to recognize the income tax on the sale of the asset. That's not ideal. The charity sold the asset, and the donor did not receive the sale proceeds. The donor would likely still be able to claim a cash charitable deduction for the value of the gift, but as we discussed above, it's not nearly as tax efficient as donating the asset themselves.

STEP 4: ACCEPT OR DECLINE RESPECTFULLY

Acceptance

Harvested crops, livestock, and machinery are transferred via a *Deed of Gift*. You will find sample deeds of gift for each of these three asset types at the end of this chapter. **They are samples.** I recommend having your legal counsel review them and, if necessary, edit to meet your state's legal requirements. Further, the donor and/or her legal advisors may wish to use their own form or edit the sample you provide to them.

Let the donor know what you will do with the gift once it's received. It's important to be transparent with donors. If your gift acceptance policies require you to sell immediately and reinvest into a board-approved investment portfolio, make sure you say so. Whatever your intent, let the donor know what will happen to their gift after receipt.

Declining Respectfully

If after you complete your due diligence, you determine that the gift is unacceptable for whatever reason, you'll need to decline respectfully.

The donor has offered a generous gift and it is important to acknowledge that. I recommend meeting with the donor to 1) thank them for their offer, and 2) explain *exactly why* you are unable to accept their gift. Explain in clear terms and illustrate your reasons. I also recommend explaining your decision in writing and giving it to the donor so they can refer back to it later.

If the donor really cares for your organization, they should understand why you must decline. They may decide to consider donating a different asset that brings you less risk.

STEP 5: MANAGE OR LIQUIDATE

In virtually all cases, you'll want to liquidate these assets. If you operate something like a farm machinery museum or your organization engages in farming, you may want to keep a piece of machinery or some livestock.

As we discussed above, the farmer will usually deliver the assets to a seller (elevator, sale barn, auctioneer) and the sale will happen very soon after the gift is made. These sellers make it pretty easy for the charity to liquidate. Just be sure you speak with the seller and make sure they understand the procedures necessary to make sure that any charitable deduction is protected. Make sure they understand that the gift and the sale are two separate transactions. The donor makes the gift and then the CHARITY controls all aspects of the sale.

Sale barns and machinery auctioneers will have an auction agreement for you to review and sign. Make sure you understand all elements of the agreement and ask as many questions as you need to so that you know the sale will work.

If the assets are sold within 3 years of the gift, the charity must file IRS Form 8282 with the IRS. This form lets the IRS know how much the assets were sold for. The IRS matches the 8282 with the 8283 filed by the donor to compare the deduction the donor took with the ultimate sale price of the gift. If the assets were sold for substantially less than the deduction value claimed by the donor, it is likely the donor could face an audit of that gift. That is one reason the charity should try to get the highest and best value when selling the assets. **They should not feel compelled to sell to anyone for a discounted price or at unreasonably favorable terms.** An audit by the IRS could view this as "private benefit" on the part of the charity and the company. *Private benefit* can come with stiff financial penalties (25% excise tax, for example) for the company, the donor, the charity, employees, and board members of the charity who were involved in the transaction. The charity's nonprofit status can also be revoked in serious cases of private benefit.

SPECIAL CONSIDERATIONS FOR GIFTS OF AGRICULTURAL ASSETS TO FUND CHARITABLE GIFT ANNUITIES OR CHARITABLE REMAINDER TRUSTS

Charitable Gift Annuities

Accepting a gift of harvested crops, livestock, or machinery in exchange for a Charitable Gift Annuity (CGA) can be a risky business. When a charity enters into a CGA agreement with a donor, it is agreeing to make fixed payments to the annuitant(s) for life. The payment obligation is a general debt of the charity. As long as the charity has assets, the payments must be made. If the charity accepts an asset to fund an immediate CGA and then it takes some time to sell, the charity must dip into its own reserves to make those payments. Furthermore, gift annuity payments are based upon the value of the property when it is donated, regardless of how much it sells for. If it sells for less than the value at the time of the gift, the charity will still have to make payments based on that higher amount.

Here's an example:

Machinery value at time of gift: $350,000
ACGA immediate CGA rate for the income beneficiary: 6%
Annual Payments: $350,000 x 6% = **$21,000**
Net Machinery Sales Proceeds: $300,000
$300,000 x 6% = $18,000
Charity makes up difference of $3,000/year

If the donor lives another 20 years, that's a difference of **$60,000 the charity must cover from their own reserves.**

It is possible to accept illiquid assets like crops, livestock, and machinery in exchange for a CGA, but you should be aware of the risks when you are creating your policies.

Some charities attempt to mitigate these risks by offering a rate slightly lower than the standard ACGA[24] rate. Additionally, some only issue *deferred* gift annuity agreements in exchange for illiquid assets. That allows the charity time to sell the asset before they have to begin making payments.

You'll have to decide for yourself whether you're willing to accept agricultural assets to fund a gift annuity. If you ultimately decide it is too risky, you could seek out another provider who is willing to issue the gift annuity and then pass all or a majority of the residuum to your organization at the end of the CGA.

It's best to explore all options ahead of time so that you are prepared when someone inquires about donating an illiquid asset in exchange for a CGA. You don't want to have to figure out your options in the moment. Create your own policies and partner with another provider to facilitate gifts that carry more risk than you are comfortable carrying yourself.

Another option is to talk to the donor about using the asset to fund a Charitable Remainder Trust instead. That solution takes virtually all the risk off the charity. They aren't on the hook to make payments, invest the sales proceeds, or perform administration. The trustee of the CRT is responsible for all of that.

The main concerns from the charity's perspective are:

A. The donor can retain the ability to change the charitable beneficiaries in the CRT agreement; and

B. The donor may likely name more than one charitable beneficiary and that could lessen your ultimate share of the gift.

These aren't significant risks and are significantly offset by eliminating all the risks associated with accepting asset to fund a CGA yourself.

Charitable Remainder Unitrust

In general, agricultural assets can be ideal gifts to donate to a CRT. The donor isn't likely to receive much of a deduction (as we outlined above), but the CRT trustee sells the property tax-free—leaving 100% of the net sales proceeds available to reinvest and make the trust payments to the trust beneficiary(ies).

When the CRT comes to its scheduled end, the remaining assets are distributed to the charities the donor named in the trust agreement.

Remember, if the donor's basis in the crops, livestock, or machinery is low or zero, their deduction will also be low or zero. There may be no deduction, but they will avoid

---

[24] America Council on Gift Annuities

recognizing income tax on the sale of the assets and the income tax they do have to recognize will be spread out over time as they receive payments from the CRT.

It is a best practice to utilize the *Flip Charitable Remainder Unitrust* for gifts of any illiquid asset. The *Flip* feature gives the trustee time to market and sell the property before making payments to the income beneficiaries. The *Unitrust* feature protects the trust from erosion due to potential volatility in the sales price of the property or fluctuation in the value of trust investments over time. The payments from a *Unitrust* are based on the value of the trust assets and the payment calculation is re-established every year. For example, if the *Unitrust* payment percentage is 6% and the trust asset value in year one is $100,000, the payment in that year would be $6,000.

$100,000 x 6% = $6,000

If the trust asset value is $110,000 in year two, the payment that year would be $6,600.

$110,000 x 6% = $6,600

Notice the payout percentage does not change. That is constant and is written into the trust document. The payments will fluctuate every year depending on how the trust investments perform. This provides some protection for the remainder value to charity.

A Charitable Remainder Annuity Trust (CRAT) is not recommended for gifts of illiquid assets. If it were used, the payout would be based on the payout percentage and the value of the gift on the date of the gift. If the property sells for less than the gift value and the investments perform poorly, the trust could be significantly depleted leaving little to nothing for charity at the end. Furthermore, the *Flip* feature cannot be added to a CRAT. Without that feature, the trustee would have to make payments immediately, regardless of whether the property had sold or not. If the property hasn't sold and the trust has no liquid assets, the only way to make a payment would be to deed shares of the property to the income recipient. That creates a whole host of problems that we won't go into here. Just know that when dealing with gifts of illiquid assets, the *FLIP CRUT* is the trust type of choice.

One risk that is associated with this gift comes up when charities serve as the *trustee* of a Charitable Remainder Trust. Some charities do this as a matter of practice, but you should be aware of the risks. A trustee is responsible for many things, including:
- Asset management and investment
- Annual tax filings
- Payments to human income beneficiaries
- Protecting assets for the human and charitable beneficiaries

Litigation is not uncommon. The human or charitable beneficiaries may feel the trustee has mismanaged the assets or misreported data on the tax filings and could file a lawsuit. Furthermore, these are *tax-exempt* trusts. The IRS keeps a very close eye on them.

A trustee is considered a *fiduciary*. Fiduciaries have a *legal* duty to protect the interests of those they are charged with protecting. In this case, it's the human and charitable beneficiaries. Violation of that duty could result in severe penalties for the trustee as an organization or for the individual at the organization who is in charge of managing the trust.

Think twice before agreeing to serve as trustee of a Charitable Remainder Trust. Understand all the risks and get professional legal guidance before you do it.

Sample Harvested Crops Gift Procedures

1. Conduct initial conversations with donor about gift basics.

2. Provide donor with *Gift of Harvested Crops Instructions* and *Deed of Gift* form.

3. Donor delivers crops to elevator along with a *copy* of completed *Deed of Gift* form.

4. Donor mails the completed original *Deed of Gift* form to charity AND contacts charity to notify them the crops has been dropped off at elevator.

5. Charity contacts elevator to order sale of crops and requests check be mailed or money wired to charity.

6. Charity sends the donor a written acknowledgment of the gift.

Sample Harvested Crops Gift Instructions

Donors should consult their tax and legal advisors prior to making a gift in order to fully understand all financial and tax consequences.

Donors should carefully follow the steps outlined below to protect any potential tax benefits of making the gift.

Steps to Making a Gift of Crops

1. Donor delivers crops and <u>copy</u> of the completed *Deed of Gift Form* to a grain elevator in the name of _____.
2. The donor should NOT instruct nor advise the elevator to sell the crops.
3. Donor contacts charity to let them know the crops have been delivered to the elevator.
4. Donor mails completed <u>*original*</u> *Deed of Gift* form to <u>charity</u> at:

    _____

    _____

    _____

5. Charity will contact the elevator to request sale of crops and proceeds transferred to charity.
6. Charity will send a written acknowledgment of the gift to donor.

Sample **Harvested Crops Deed of Gift**

I/We _____give

_____ bushels of _____

to _____.

☐ I/We verify this gift of crops has no liens against it.

☐ I/We verify this gift of crops did have a lien against it, but it has been removed as evidenced by the attached lien waiver executed by the lender.

_____

Signature   Date

_____

Printed Name

This gift of harvested crops was delivered to:

Elevator Name: _____

Elevator Contact Name, Address and Phone:

_____

_____

_____

Please mail the original of this form to:

_____

_____

_____

_____

Sample Livestock Gift Procedures

1. Conduct initial conversations with donor about gift basics.

2. Donor and charity discuss timing of donation and coordinate with sale barn.

3. Send Donor the *Livestock Gift Instructions* and *Deed of Gift* form.

4. Donor delivers livestock to sale barn along with a <u>copy</u> of completed *Deed of Gift* form. Donor contacts charity to notify of delivery.

5. Donor mails original completed *Deed of Gift* form to charity.

6. Charity discusses sale particulars with sale barn and sale occurs.

7. Sale barn sends sales proceeds charity.

8. Send donor a written acknowledgment of the gift.

Sample Livestock Gift Instructions

Donors should consult their tax and legal advisors prior to making a gift in order to fully understand all financial and tax consequences.

Donors should carefully follow the steps outlined below to protect any potential tax benefits of making the gift.

Steps to Making a Gift of Livestock

1. Donor delivers livestock and <u>copy</u> of the completed *Deed of Gift* form to the sale barn in the name of _____.

2. The donor should NOT instruct nor advise the sale barn to sell the livestock.

3. Donor contacts charity to notify them that livestock have been delivered.

4. Donor mails original completed *Deed of Gift* form to charity at:

    _____

    _____

    _____

    _____

5. Charity will contact the sale barn to request sale of livestock.

Sample Livestock Deed of Gift

I/We _____ give

_____ head of _____ to

_____.

☐ I/We verify this gift of livestock has no liens against it.

☐ I/We verify this gift of livestock did have a lien against it, but it has been removed as evidenced by the attached lien waiver executed by the lender.

_____

Signature   Date

_____

Printed Name

This gift of livestock was delivered to:

Sale Barn Name: _____

Sale Barn Contact Name, Address and Phone:

_____

_____

_____

Please mail this completed original form to:

_____

_____

_____

_____

Sample Farm Machinery Gift Procedures

1. Conduct initial conversation with donor about gift basics.

2. Donor completes and returns the *Farm Machinery Gift Questionnaire.*

3. Donor and charity discuss timing of donation and charity coordinates details of sale with auctioneer.

4. Send donor the *Farm Machinery Gift Instructions* and *Deed of Gift* form.

5. Donor delivers machinery along with a <u>copy</u> of completed *Deed of Gift* form to the auctioneer.

6. Donor contacts charity to notify of delivery to auctioneer's sale lot.

7. Donor mails *original* completed *Deed of Gift* form to charity.

8. Send the donor a written acknowledgment of the gift.

9. Charity finalizes sale details with auctioneer and auction occurs.

10. Auctioneer sends sales proceeds to charity.

Sample Farm Machinery Gift Questionnaire

1. What type of farm machinery would you like to donate? Please list type and vehicle identification number(s), if possible.

    _____
    _____
    _____

2. When would you like to make the donation?

    _____

3. What auctioneer do you usually work with and where is it located?

    _____
    _____
    _____

4. What is the approximate value of the machinery you wish to donate? Please list items separately.

    _____
    _____
    _____
    _____

5. Are you under contract to sell this machinery to anyone and/or for a specific price? YES NO

Please contact us right away with any questions or concerns you have about this questionnaire. We want you to be absolutely comfortable with your proposed gift. We also want to create an open conversation with you and your advisors about why this information is needed and how it will be used.

I understand that the truth and accuracy of my answers to the previous questions will be relied upon when evaluating my proposed gift of farm machinery. I certify that each of the answers is true, accurate, and complete to the best of my knowledge.

_____   _____
Signature   Date

_____   _____
Printed name   Phone Number

Sample Farm Machinery Gift Instructions

Donors should consult their tax and legal advisors prior to making a gift in order to fully understand all financial and tax consequences.

Donors should carefully follow the steps outlined below to protect any potential tax benefits of making the gift.

Steps to Making a Gift of Farm Machinery

1. Donor delivers machinery and <u>copy</u> of the completed *Deed of Gift* form to the auctioneer in the name of the charity. *Please use separate Deed of Gift documents for each piece of machinery being donated.*
2. The donor should NOT instruct, nor advise the auctioneer to sell the machinery.
3. Donor contacts charity to notify the machinery has been delivered.
4. Donor mails <u>*original*</u> completed *Deed of Gift* form(s) to charity at:

   _____

   _____

   _____

5. Charity will coordinate with the auctioneer for the sale of the machinery and check mailed to charity.
6. Charity will send a written acknowledgment of the gift to donor.

Sample Farm Machinery Deed of Gift

I/We _____give

_____

_____, with Vehicle ID Number _____

to _____.

    ☐ I/We verify this gift of machinery has no liens against it.

    ☐ I/We verify this gift of machinery did have a lien against it, but it has been removed as evidenced by the attached lien waiver executed by the lender.

_____

Signature   Date

_____

Printed name

This gift of machinery was delivered to:

Auctioneer Name: _____

Auctioneer Contact Name, Address and Phone:

_____

_____

_____

Please mail this original completed form to:

_____

_____

_____

Chapter 7:
Gifts of Closely Held Stock

In Chapter 2 we went through Publicly traded Stock, Mutual Funds, and ETFs. Now it's time to look at Closely Held Stock. It's very important to understand the difference. Publicly traded Securities are traded on a public market like the New York Stock Exchange, Shenzhen Stock Exchange of China, and the Toronto Stock Exchange of Canada. Most countries have a public stock exchange. Virtually anyone can purchase stock available at these exchanges.

Closely Held Stock is not traded on an exchange. It is owned by an exclusive list of people—often members of just one family. These companies are referred to as "private" or "closely held" because their bylaws restrict ownership to a set group of people. These companies are often smaller than public stock companies, but not always. Sometimes they are massive global enterprises.

Shareholders of these companies sometimes donate shares of their "private" companies to charity. That's an exciting thing!

Entrepreneurs are the most generous segment of American society. A study by Fidelity Charitable[25] outlines several ways they outpace their non-entrepreneur peers when it comes to philanthropy.

- Entrepreneurs give 50% more to charity than non-entrepreneurs.
- Nearly twice as many consider giving a "very high financial priority".
- 69% say they want to incorporate charitable giving into their exit plans.

Let's apply our 5-Step process to Closely Held Stock to discover the opportunities it brings and how it differs from a gift of Public Securities. At the end of this chapter, you will find *Sample Procedures* and a *Closely Held Stock Gift Questionnaire*. These documents are meant to help you get started. You will definitely want to edit them to meet your organization's specific needs.

---

[25] *Entrepreneurs as Philanthropists: Understanding Entrepreneurs' Unique Approach to Giving*, Fidelity Charitable, 2018.

1. **Know the Basics**
2. **Ask for the Right Information**
3. **Evaluate for Opportunity and Risk**
4. **Accept or Decline Respectfully**
5. **Manage or Liquidate**

STEP 1: KNOW THE BASICS

Thankfully, many of the tax rules for Closely held stock are pretty much identical when it comes to donations to charity. Closely held stock is a capital asset and it comes with the same favorable tax treatment as other capital assets like real estate and public stock. Let's review.

When you give a capital asset like Closely Held stock, the income tax deduction is based on the fair market value of the shares on the day of the gift, regardless of what you paid for it (as long as it's been owned for at least a year and a day). Simply put, if you paid $5.00 for a share of stock 10 years ago and today it's worth $25.00, your deduction for a gift of that share of stock would be $25.00. That's basically $20.00 of deduction for FREE! Additionally, you avoid recognition of the capital gain when the gift is made. That means you don't have to pay capital gains tax like you would if you sold the stock. When it comes to charitable deductions, not all assets receive this special treatment. **Only long-term capital assets qualify for this exceptional double benefit.**

If you sell the stock and donate the cash, you don't avoid the capital gains tax. Sure, you would be entitled to a charitable income tax deduction for the cash gift, but that extra capital gains income can cause a ripple effect in your tax picture. For example, extra income can increase the tax paid on Social Security income or increase Medicare premiums. Charitable deductions don't have any effect on those increases. **In the end, it's much more efficient to give the stock itself.**

The donor will need to acquire a *Qualified Appraisal* of the shares to deter-mine the value for charitable deduction purposes. *Qualified Appraisals* require specific elements and are outlined in IRS Publications 526 and 561. Publicly traded stock does not require an appraisal, because the value is easy to determine. The shares trade frequently on an open market and so the value is more easily calculated. Closely held stock does not sell frequently; therefore, the rules require an appraisal to determine their value. These appraisals can be quite expensive—sometimes up to 1-2% of the value of the whole business. The appraisal cost is sometimes cost-prohibitive, and the donor may decide to sell the business and make a cash gift from the proceeds instead. It's smart for them to consider both options to determine the best choice for their situation.

The appraiser is likely to apply a "discount" to the value of the shares. There are two primary types of discounts that they may apply. First, is the *lack of marketability discount*. Since there is a small number of people who are permitted to own the stock, the market for sale is limited. Therefore, the value of the stock can be reduced for appraisal purposes. The second type is a *minority discount*. If the shareholder owns a minority ownership share, she won't have as much power over the decisions being made by the company. Her shares aren't worth quite as much as someone who owns a *majority* share, because that majority owner will have more power. Votes of the majority owner carry more weight. The more shares you own, the more power your votes have. That's the simple math behind shareholder voting.

Gifts of Closely held stock tend to come at a specific time in a person's life. At some point they will want to exit the business. Most people who own Closely held stock work for the company. It's often been their life's work to build and grow the company, but at some point they'll be ready to retire. They may wish to sell the business to a new owner OR give/sell it to heirs. This time of transition is most often when they will consider donating shares of the business to charity. This is one of the "life events" we looked at in Chapter 1.

The sale of their business will probably be the biggest "taxable event" of their lives. When they sell the stock or underlying assets of the business, they will probably recognize a LOT of taxable income. As I always say,

"Taxes don't define the WHY of the gift, but they very often determine the WHEN of the gift."

This large taxable event will be their opportunity to give more to charity than they ever thought possible. Furthermore, donating the Closely held stock to charity prior to a business sale may offer them significant tax savings—as opposed to selling the business and then donating cash.

These business transition plans often take years to plan. That's why it's very important to start the giving conversation early on in your relationship with a business owner. If the transition plan is designed without any consideration given to charitable giving, it can quickly become too late to add that charitable component back in. Business owners don't automatically think of donating stock to charity prior to exiting the business and neither do their advisors. **It's our job as fundraisers to plant that seed early so the option can at least be considered. The donor deserves to know all their options going into the planning process.**

Closely held stock comes in a variety of forms. We're going to look at the four most common types you're likely to encounter (C corps, S corps, Limited Liability Companies, and Partnerships) and analyze each one within Steps 2-5.

Regardless of which type you're dealing with, there are always some basic questions to consider at the outset.

- What does the donor own?
- What can the donor give?
- What liability comes with the shares?
- What risk comes with the shares?
- What is the charity's exit plan?

What does the donor own?

In many cases I've dealt with, the donor wishes to donate an asset of the company, such as a piece of real estate. If she is the sole owner of the business, she may consider herself the owner of the business assets as well. That isn't the case. She owns shares in the business. The business owns the assets. It's important to remember that if the business assets (like real estate, machinery, inventory) are donated, the business will be the donor—not the individual. That can make a significant difference in the financial benefit of the gift to the donor. Sometimes it's the best choice for the donor, but details of both options (gift of stock vs. gift of assets) should be thoroughly examined by her advisors.

You should take caution if the company wishes to donate "all or substantially all" of its assets to charity. That could be treated as an asset liquidation by the IRS and the company could be forced to recognize income on the value of the assets even though it was the charity that ultimately sold them. "All or substantially all" is a vague term, but that is the standard used. Be wary of any situation where a closely held company wishes to donate a substantial amount of its assets to charity *and* make sure you encourage the donor to receive experienced legal and tax advice before proceeding.

What can the donor give?

Many closely held businesses adopt "Buy-Sell Agreements" or "Cross-Purchase Agreements". These documents outline who can own shares of the business and under what circumstances shares can or must be sold. That's how they keep the shares from being sold to anyone outside the pre-established group. Most agreements that I've encountered don't specifically allow for a charity to be a shareholder. If that's the case, the company will probably need to amend the buy-sell/cross-purchase agreement to allow for donations of shares to charity. To do that, the shareholders will have to agree to make that change. If the donor is the only owner, it should be pretty easy to make that change.

What liability comes with the shares?

Depending on the way the business is incorporated, shares given to charity come with different levels of risk (legal, financial, etc.). We will take a look at the different risks that come with C corps, S corps, and Limited Liability Companies, and Partnerships in Step 3.

There is an important liability situation to be aware of when it comes to income tax imposed upon charities that own closely held stock. It's called "Unrelated Business Taxable Income" (UBTI). When charities own part or all of a business that is *unrelated* to its mission, the charity can be subject to UBTI and the rate is quite high. It's equal the highest corporate tax rate—whatever that happens to be at the time. There is a reason behind UBTI. Congress doesn't want charities operating commercial businesses and avoiding income tax due to their tax-exempt status. It would give them an unfair advantage over for-profit businesses. Charities can operate income tax-exempt businesses that further their mission. A good example is a charity that works to help people in third-world countries earn a living wage operating a "fair trade" farm and selling the produce.

It is worth noting that a charity organized as a trust, rather than a corporation, may not be subject to UBTI. That is a very advanced area of charitable tax law, and we won't discuss it in detail in this book.

What is the charity's exit plan?

The vast majority of charities do not want to be a long-term shareholder of a closely held business. They want to liquidate the shares as soon as possible after receiving them and apply the sales proceeds to their mission. Since the shares aren't sold on a public exchange and can only be owned by a set number of individuals, the market for sale is limited. There may not be an interested buyer for the shares at any given time. Therefore, the charity needs to assess the marketability of the shares prior to accepting the gift. We will look at this in more detail in Step 2.

STEP 2: ASK FOR THE RIGHT INFORMATION

You'll need to collect a wide variety of information for a gift of closely held stock. The *Closely Held Stock Gift Questionnaire* at the end of this chapter covers quite a wide range of information. Here, we will take a look at some of the more important items of note.

The business incorporation type is quite important. That will determine the kinds of risks that come with the stock. We'll take a closer look at risk in Step 3.

You'll want to know the estimated value of the shares to determine if it meets your gift minimum. Many charities set a higher gift minimum for donations of closely held stock than they do for public stock. That's because these gifts require a great deal more due diligence work on the part of the charity.

As we discussed earlier, marketability is of the utmost importance. You'll want to know how quickly the shares can be sold after the gift is made. That being said, both you and the donor should be wary of any prearranged sale situations. If the donor has been discussing a sale or entered into a sale agreement with a potential buyer, that could be deemed a prearranged sale and significantly affect the donor's charitable deduction.

Prearranged sales can be a gray area of the law. Not all authorities agree on the definition of what a prearranged sale looks like. Court cases, tax code, and IRS opinions differ. One thing we know for sure is that if the IRS audits a donor's gift and determines the ultimate sale of the shares by the charity was arranged prior to the gift, the donor will likely have to recognize the capital gains on the sale. They should still be entitled to a charitable deduction for an equivalent cash gift, but as we outlined earlier in this chapter that won't be as tax efficient as a deduction for the value of the shares.

Even if the business isn't subject to an agreement to sell, the shareholders may have decided they wish to sell. Generally, once the shareholders have voted to sell the business, a donor is no longer able to avoid the capital gains tax on the sale of her shares—even if she donates them prior to the sale. This is because of something called "Assignment of Income". At the time of the shareholder vote in favor of a sale, the shareholders are likely legally obligated to sell their shares to the new buyer—even if there is no purchase agreement in place. If someone donates shares to charity, the charity will also be obligated to sell to the new buyer. Therefore, the donor would probably have to recognize the capital gain on the sale but would likely be entitled to a deduction for the cash value of the shares. I've worked on several cases where shareholders have voted to sell their shares to a new buyer. At that point, all shareholders were legally obligated to sell and someone wanted to avoid the associated capital gains. They wonder if donating the shares to charity before the sale takes place would avoid the tax. It won't—IF the shareholders have already voted to sell. **As you can see, it is ESSENTIAL that donors engage qualified legal and tax counsel if they are considering a gift of closely held stock.**

Needless to say, it is VERY important to sniff out any potential prearranged sales before the gift discussion goes too far.

You'll certainly want to review corporate documents and financials, such as Bylaws, tax returns, Articles of Incorporation, etc. You'll want to know exactly what you're getting into, and these documents go a long way to disclose how the business operates as well as its financial situation.

STEP 3: EVALUATE FOR OPPORTUNITY AND RISK

Closely held stock can be VERY valuable and bring with it wonderful financial opportunity for a charity, but it also comes with risks. Don't be seduced by the value of the gift to the point you take on more risk than you're able to manage.

Each type of closely held stock brings different types of risk; therefore, we're going to review them one at a time.

The type of stock (C corp, S corp, Limited Liability Company, Partnership) just refers to how the company is incorporated. Different company types come with different legal and taxation rules for the company and the shareholders. The owners will choose the incorporation type that best meets its needs.

C Corporation

C corps tend to be larger companies (100+ employees). Shareholders do not take on any legal or financial liability when they own shares. This means that C corp stock is generally the least risky type for charities to accept. The value of the stock will rise and fall, but the charity won't be responsible for the company's debts or legal obligations. The primary risk to the charity will be the fluctuation in stock price.

C corps are subject to something called "double taxation". That means that the company pays income tax on its earnings AND shareholders pay income tax on income they receive from their shares. Income from shares is called a "dividend". *Double taxation* is rather unique to C corps. From the charity's perspective, this doesn't matter much. They are exempt from income tax for the most part. If a charity owns C corp stock and receives dividends, it won't likely have to pay any income tax.

Another tax advantage is that C corp shares aren't usually subject to UBTI, so that risk is significantly lessened for the charity.

Most of the time, the biggest risk charities face when they accept closely held C corp stock is the time it takes to sell. Is the stock marketable and how long will it take to sell? Most charity boards of directors outline an investment policy that will require the charity to sell all non-cash gifts as soon as possible and either spend the proceeds on their mission OR invest in an approved portfolio.

Closely held stock can take a while to sell if there are no interested buyers. That means the charity is stuck with the shares for an unknown period of time. It's not the end of the world, but the value can fluctuate greatly over time—up or down.

The charity will also have to ascertain the value of the shares every year for its 990 Federal Tax Return. Determining that value can be expensive and labor-intensive.

The C corp itself can donate its assets to charity. Sometimes this is a more advantageous option for the owners of the company and the charity. A shareholder may not wish to donate her stock, but the company may have an asset—such as a piece of real estate—that it wishes to donate. The real estate may be more readily marketable than the shares of stock because it can be sold to anyone. Ownership of the stock is restricted to the limited number of people outlined in the corporate documents, but corporate assets can typically be given or sold to anyone.

S Corporation

S corps tend to be smaller companies. By law, they cannot have more than 100 shareholders. S corps are subject to a "single level" of taxation. Unlike a C corp, the S corp does not pay tax at the corporate level. All taxable income is "passed through" to the shareholders and they report it on their tax returns. Shareholders are generally shielded from personal liability for corporate debts and legal obligations. Therefore, a charity owner of S corp stock should have that same protection from liability.

The charity is very likely to be subject to UBTI on dividends AND on gain from the sale of shares. Again, that UBTI rate is equal to whatever the highest corporate income tax rate is at the time. I've seen situations where the charity would be subject to higher taxation (because of UBTI) on a gift of S corp stock than the donor would if she sold the stock herself. In those cases, the donors were inclined to sell the stock and make a subsequent gift of cash. It resulted in less tax liability and therefore a larger charitable gift.

Just like any type of closely held stock gift—a significant risk to the charity is the time it takes to sell the stock. Are there any interested buyers? How might the share price fluctuate between the gift date and the ultimate sale of the shares? In the meantime, the charity could be subject to significant tax on income from the shares.

An S corp can donate cash or its assets to charity. Those assets are likely not be subject to UBTI and therefore could be a more tax-efficient gift. Additionally, the charity could sell the assets to virtually anyone. The pool of potential buyers is almost definitely larger. The shares are still subject to the corporate rules limiting *who* is permitted to own shares. In the case of an asset donation, the deduction would be passed along to all shareholders according to their ownership share.

Limited Liability Company (LLC)

LLCs tend to be smaller companies. Some have only one "member"/owner. LLCs do not issue stock, but rather "membership interests". If someone wants to contribute her ownership shares to charity, she will be donating *membership interests.*

LLCs are relatively easy to establish and subject to a "single level" of taxation—like S corps. Taxable income is "passed through" to the shareholders and they report it on their tax returns. **A charity owner of LLC interests would likely be subject to UBTI on income received, but *not* on capital gain from sale of the interests.**

Members' personal assets are generally shielded from legal liability for the company's actions, but company debts do come along with the ownership interest. **Therefore, a charity owner would be taking on a share of the company's debts if it accepts the membership interests.** When a donor contributes debt-encumbered property to a charity, it is considered a "Bargain Sale". That means that the donor will likely need to recognize income in the amount of the outstanding debt passed along to the charity through the gift.

When LLCs need cash to cover expenses, they will sometimes issue "capital calls". A capital call is a requirement for members to contribute cash to the company. A charity member/owner would not be exempt from capital calls. **If any are issued during the charity's term as owner, it would be required to contribute cash to the company.** Therefore, you'll definitely want to know if any capital calls are expected in the future.

As with all gifts of closely held stock, the charity should be thinking about its exit plan early on. How long will it take to liquidate the shares/membership interests? Is there a market for sale? **Holding period can be the biggest risk for charities—especially if it is going to be subject to potential capital calls and company debts.**

In some cases, it may be simpler for the LLC to donate cash or assets itself—rather than a member contributing her membership interests. That would likely eliminate UBTI concerns. It would eliminate the need for an expensive appraisal of the business and discounts for minority ownership or lack of marketability would not be applied to an appraisal of assets. The charitable deduction would "flow through" to all of the members to report on their tax returns.

Partnership

Partnership interests come in two varieties—*General* and *Limited*. Partnerships *must* have a General partner and *may* have Limited partners—if there is more than one owner.

A *General* partner is involved in day-to-day operations of the partnership and is subject to both legal liability and company debts. *Limited* partners are subject to company debts, but not legal liability. **It is a best practice NOT to accept gifts of *General* partnership interests.** They come with more liability AND greater responsibility. Remember, the General partner runs the business operations. A charity is probably not interested in running a business.

Just like LLCs, **Partnership interests come along with company debts.** A charity owner would not be exempt from that. **The Bargain Sale rules apply to gifts of Partnership interests subject to debt.** The Bargain Sale is described above in the LLC section.

Capital calls are a concern with Partnerships. Those are described above within the LLC section, but basically they are requirements for owners to contribute cash to the Partnership.

In some cases, it may be simpler for the Partnership to donate cash or assets itself—rather than a partner contributing her partnership interests. That would likely eliminate UBTI concerns. It would eliminate the need for an expensive appraisal of the business and discounts for minority ownership or lack of marketability would not be applied to an appraisal of assets. The charitable deduction would "flow through" to all of the partners to report on their tax returns.

STEP 4: ACCEPT OR DECLINE RESPECTFULLY

Once you've completed your due diligence, you'll have to decide if the gift of closely held stock is worth the associated risks. If not, you should have a candid conversation with the donor and communicate *exactly WHY* you've decided to decline. It's a good practice to communicate your reasons verbally AND on paper. That way, the donor can easily refer back to it and use it to clearly explain to her advisors why the gift was declined. If she really cares about your organization, she will understand and possibly consider a different kind of gift—one that doesn't bring as much risk.

If the gift poses more risk than you are able to accept, you may not have to decline the gift. You may be able to work with another organization to accept it on your behalf. Many community foundations and commercial Donor Advised Fund providers are experts at accepting these more complex assets. They may be able to lend a hand and make the gift possible.

If you decide to accept the asset, you'll then move on to the transfer of ownership. If the stock/interests are held in certificate form, the donor will need to execute a stock power form and deliver with certificates to the charity to transfer ownership. The company will then need to issue new certificates in the name of the charity. If held electronically, work with the holding company and donor to execute transfer of ownership.

As discussed earlier, if the donor wishes to take a charitable deduction for the gift of shares/interests and they are worth more than $5,000, she will need to acquire a *Qualified Appraisal* of the shares/interests. In addition, she will need to file IRS Form 8283 with her tax return. It must be signed by the appraiser, donor, and charity. The charity's signature is not to verify the value of the gift, but rather to attest to the fact that they received the gift of that particular asset on a particular date. The charity should NOT complete the form for the donor and should only sign *after* the form has been completed and signed by both the appraiser and donor.

No matter the type of gift, it is very important to communicate your gift acceptance process with the donor.

Let them know what you will do with the gift once it's received. It's important to be transparent with donors. If your gift acceptance policies require you to sell immediately and reinvest into a board-approved investment portfolio, make sure you say so. Whatever your intent, let the donor know what will happen to their gift after receipt.

Let them know how/when you will send them a gift receipt. In order to take a tax deduction for a gift of stock, the donor will need a gift receipt from you.

STEP 5: MANAGE OR LIQUIDATE

Once ownership has transferred, you will either hold and manage the shares/interests OR liquidate them. Most charities will lean toward liquidation.

Discuss with the donor the method of sale. Get her input, since she knows the business better than anyone else. See if she can provide a list of interested buyers, including the corporation itself. If the company has an Investor Relations department, it can be helpful.

Agreements to sell should be in writing. A trusted banker can be helpful to hold payment in escrow. It is a best practice that the charity NOT "finance" the sale, but in some cases I have seen charities accept a *promissory note* for the shares and accept payment over time. You'll want to understand all the potential accounting, tax, and financial ramifications of accepting a promissory note in lieu of cash payment.

If the shares/interests are sold within 3 years of the gift, the charity must file IRS Form 8282 with the IRS. This form lets the IRS know how much the shares/interests were sold for. The IRS matches the 8282 with the 8283 filed by the donor to compare the deduction the donor took with the ultimate sale price of the gift. If the shares/interests were sold for substantially less than the deduction value claimed by the donor, it is likely the donor could face an audit of that gift. That is one reason the charity should try to get the highest and best value when selling the shares/interests. **They should not feel compelled to sell to anyone for a discounted price or at unreasonably favorable terms.** An audit by the IRS could view this as "private benefit" on the part of the charity and the company. *Private benefit* can come with stiff financial penalties (25% excise tax, for example) for the company, the donor, the charity, employees, and board members of the charity who were involved in the transaction. The charity's nonprofit status can also be revoked in serious cases of private benefit.

SPECIAL CONSIDERATIONS FOR GIFTS OF CLOSELY HELD STOCK TO FUND CHARITABLE GIFT ANNUITIES OR CHARITABLE REMAINDER TRUSTS

Closely held stock can be an acceptable gift type for contribution to a Charitable Remainder Unitrust (CRUT). It is not particularly advisable to fund a Charitable Gift Annuity (CGA), nor a Charitable Remainder Annuity Trust (CRAT). The CRUT can be outfitted with a "Flip" provision that allows the trustee time to sell the donated assets before having to start making payments to the CRUT income beneficiaries. That is especially helpful when the only thing donated to the trust are illiquid assets that will take time to sell. Both the CRAT and the *Immediate* Gift Annuity require payments to begin to the income beneficiaries right away—typically within one calendar quarter or, at most, a year. If the assets aren't sold before the income start date, the trustee will be required to transfer portions of the donated assets back to the income beneficiaries. That isn't what anyone wants—for a variety of reasons we won't go into here.

If the charity accepts an asset to fund a CGA and it takes some time to sell, the charity must dip into its own reserves to make those payments. Furthermore, gift annuity payments are based upon the value of the property when it is donated, regardless of how much it sells for. If it sells for less than the value at the time of the gift, the charity will still have to make payments based on that higher amount.

Here's an example:

Stock value at time of gift: $350,000
ACGA immediate CGA rate for the income beneficiary: 6%
Annual Payments: $350,000 x 6% = **$21,000**
Net Sales Proceeds: $300,000
$300,000 x 6% = $18,000
Charity makes up difference of $3,000/year

If the donor lives another 20 years, that's a difference of **$60,000 the charity must cover from their own reserves.**

It is possible to accept closely held stock in exchange for a CGA, but you should be aware of the risks when you are creating your policies.

Some charities attempt to mitigate these risks by offering a rate slightly lower than the standard ACGA[26] rate. Additionally, some only issue *deferred* gift annuity agreements in exchange for illiquid assets. That allows the charity time to sell the asset before they have to begin making payments.

You'll have to decide for yourself whether you're willing to accept closely held stock to fund a gift annuity. If you ultimately decide it is too risky, you could seek out another provider who is willing to issue the gift annuity and then pass all or a majority of the residuum to your organization at the end of the CGA.

It's best to explore all options ahead of time so that you are prepared when someone inquires about donating an illiquid asset in exchange for a CGA. You don't want to have to figure out your options in the moment. Create your own policies and partner with another provider to facilitate gifts that carry more risk than you are comfortable carrying yourself.

Another option is to talk to the donor about using the asset to fund a Charitable Remainder Trust instead. That solution takes virtually all the risk off the charity. They aren't on the hook to make payments, invest the sales proceeds, or perform administration. The trustee of the CRT is responsible for all of that.

The main concerns from the charity's perspective are:

    A.   The donor can retain the ability to change the charitable beneficiaries in the CRT agreement; and

    B.   The donor may likely name more than one charitable beneficiary and that could lessen your ultimate share of the gift.

These aren't significant risks and are significantly offset by eliminating all the risks associated with accepting asset to fund a CGA yourself.

---

[26] America Council on Gift Annuities

Charitable Remainder Unitrust

In general, closely held stock can be a good gift to donate to a CRT. The donor receives a charitable income tax deduction based upon the appraised value of the stock. The CRT trustee sells the property tax-free—leaving 100% of the net sales proceeds available to reinvest and make the trust payments to the trust beneficiary(ies). When the CRT comes to its scheduled end, the remaining assets are distributed to the charities the donor named in the trust agreement.

It is a best practice to utilize the *Flip Charitable Remainder Unitrust* for gifts of any illiquid asset. The *Flip* feature gives the trustee time to market and sell the property before making payments to the income beneficiaries. The *Unitrust* feature protects the trust from erosion due to potential volatility in the sales price of the property or fluctuation in the value of trust investments over time. The payments from a *Unitrust* are based on the value of the trust assets and the payment calculation is re-established every year. For example, if the *Unitrust* payment percentage is 6% and the trust asset value in year one is $100,000, the payment in that year would be $6,000.

$100,000 x 6% = $6,000

If the trust asset value is $110,000 in year two, the payment that year would be $6,600.

$110,000 x 6% = $6,600

Notice the payout percentage does not change. That is constant and is written into the trust document. The payments will fluctuate every year depending on how the trust assets are invested. This provides some protection for the remainder value to charity.

A Charitable Remainder Annuity Trust (CRAT) is not recommended for gifts of illiquid assets. If it were used, the payout would be based on the payout percentage and the value of the gift on the date of the gift. If the property sells for less than the gift value and the investments perform poorly, the trust could be significantly depleted, leaving little to nothing for charity at the end. Furthermore, the *Flip* feature cannot be added to a CRAT. Without that feature, the trustee would have to make payments immediately, regardless of whether the property had sold or not. If the property hasn't sold and the trust has no liquid assets, the only way to make a payment would be to deed shares of the property to the income recipient. That creates a whole host of problems that we won't go into here. Just know that when dealing with gifts of illiquid assets, the *FLIP CRUT* is the trust type of choice.

As discussed above, some closely held stock comes along with company debt. If debt-encumbered property is donated to a charity in return for a CGA, the Bargain Sale rules apply, and the donor is likely to have to recognize income in the amount of the debt. If debt-encumbered property is donated to a CRUT, the debt can be treated as UBTI and the trust could face a 100% excise tax on the UBTI amount. As discussed above, S corp stock, LLC interests, and Partnership interests can subject a charity (and a CRT) to UBTI on income and, in the case of an S corp, UBTI on capital gain from the sale of the shares. These types of UBTI in a CRT would also be subject to the same 100% tax. UBTI isn't a total barrier to the gift, but the calculations should be completed before the gift is made to determine the amount of potential tax that could be assessed to the CRT.

One risk of note is when charities serve as the *trustee* of a Charitable Remainder Trust. Some charities do this as a matter of practice, but you should be aware of the risks. A trustee is responsible for many things, including:

- Asset management and investment
- Annual tax filings
- Payments to human income beneficiaries
- Protecting assets for the human and charitable beneficiaries

Litigation is not uncommon. The human or charitable beneficiaries may feel the trustee has mismanaged the assets or misreported data on the tax filings and could file a lawsuit. Furthermore, these are *tax-exempt* trusts. The IRS keeps a very close eye on them.

A trustee is considered a *fiduciary*. Fiduciaries have a *legal* duty to protect the interests of those they are charged with protecting. In this case, it's the human and charitable beneficiaries. Violation of that duty could result in severe penalties for the trustee as an organization or for the individual at the organization who is in charge of managing the trust.

Think twice before agreeing to serve as trustee of a Charitable Remainder Trust. Understand all the risks and get professional legal guidance before you do it.

Sample Closely Held Stock Gift Procedures

1. Conduct initial conversations with donor about gift basics.

2. Donor completes and returns the *Closely Held Stock Gift Questionnaire.*

3. Review completed *Closely Held Stock Gift Questionnaire* and accompanying documentation. If documentation is missing, be sure to acquire it from donor.

4. If any red flags arise from review of *Closely Held Stock Gift Questionnaire*, discuss with donor and resolve—if possible.

5. Acquire a copy of the appraisal if it has been completed. The donor will need to get an appraisal in order to take an income tax deduction for the gift. It is to the charity's benefit to see the appraisal *before* the gift is accepted. First, it will help to know whether the gift meets the minimum gift value. Second, it will help to arrive at a reasonable sale price.

6. If no red flags exist and gift meets the minimum, begin the asset transfer. If stock is held in certificate form, the donor will need to execute a stock power form and deliver with certificates to charity to transfer ownership. If held electronically, work with holding company and donor to execute transfer of ownership to charity.

7. Once gift is complete, send donor a written acknowledgment of the gift. Charity will have to sign IRS Form 8283 if the donor wishes to take a charitable income tax deduction, but the charity should NOT complete the form for the donor. Nor should it sign before the form is completed and signed by both the donor and the appraiser.

8. Discuss with donor the method of sale. Get list of potential interested buyers, including the corporation itself.

9. Approach potential buyers with offer of sale.

10. Purchase agreements should be in writing and executed by the necessary officers of the charity and the buyer.

Sample Closely Held Stock Gift Questionnaire

Please answer the following questions to the best of your ability. Accuracy and thoroughness are vital to the proper care of your gift. Any information you share will be held in the strictest of confidence and only shared with necessary staff, legal, and tax counsel.

1. What type of stock/units would you like to donate?

_____ C Corporation

_____ S Corporation

_____ Limited Liability Company

_____ Partnership (_____ General _____ Limited)

_____ Limited Liability Partnership

_____ Other _____

2. How many shares/units would you like to donate? _____

3. What is the estimated value per share/unit? _____

4. How many total shares do you own? This includes individual ownership, ownership through a subsidiary, trust or any other entity under your control. Please list in detail the number of shares and how they are titled.

_____

_____

_____

5. How many total shares are outstanding? _____

6. Have there been any recent appraisals? If yes, please attach.

_____ Yes _____ Date

_____ No

7. Are there any current agreements for the sale of the company or its assets?

_____ Yes

_____ No

8. Have there been any conversations with interested buyers regarding sale of the company?

_____ No

_____ Yes (Please provide time frame of conversations, and name(s) of interested buyers.

_____

_____

_____

9. Do you anticipate any capital calls in the next 12-24 months?

_____ No

_____ Yes (Please attach details)

10. Is the company engaged in any reportable tax shelter transactions?

_____ No

_____ Yes (Please attach complete details)

11. Please provide copies of all the following documents that apply to the company.

_____ Articles of Incorporation

_____ Bylaws

_____ Partnership Agreement

_____ Buy-Sell Agreement/Cross-Purchase Agreement

_____ Current Shareholder List

_____ 3 Years of Financials

_____ 3 Years of Tax Returns

Please contact us right away with any questions or concerns you have about this questionnaire. We want you to be absolutely comfortable with your proposed gift. We also want to create an open conversation with you and your advisors about why this information is needed and how it will be used.

I understand that the truth and accuracy of my answers to the previous questions will be relied upon when evaluating my proposed gift of closely held stock. I certify that each of the answers is true, accurate, and complete to the best of my knowledge.

_____   _____
Signature   Date

_____   _____
Print name   Phone Number

Chapter 8:
Gifts of Tangible Property

Tangible property is our "stuff". It's things we can see and touch and move around. It's not attached to land like a building. It's portable. We're talking about things like:

- Artwork
- Antiques
- Coins
- Jewelry
- Books
- Wine
- Musical Instruments
- Vehicles

Some of this "stuff" can be extremely valuable and make wonderful gifts. Some of it is valuable only to the current owner. It may hold great sentimental value to them, but not much financial value on the open market. Knowing the difference is sometimes obvious; other times, it's less apparent and will require a bit more investigation.

Let's apply our handy *5-Step Process* to Tangible Property. We're going to look at vehicles separately within each step, because they come with some special elements. At the end of this chapter, you will find *Sample Tangible Property Gift Procedures,* and a *Tangible Property Gift Questionnaire.* These documents are meant to get you started. You will definitely want to edit them to meet your organization's specific needs. You will also find a *Sample Deed of Gift* form. It is a sample. You'll want to have it edited by your outside counsel to make sure it meets with your state's legal requirements. Furthermore, your donor's advisors may wish to edit it and/or use their own form.

1. **Know the Basics**
2. **Ask for the Right Information**
3. **Evaluate for Opportunity and Risk**
4. **Accept or Decline Respectfully**
5. **Manage or Liquidate**

STEP 1: KNOW THE BASICS

First, let's go through the tax basics of Tangible Property. It is considered a Capital Gain asset, unless it's inventory from a business. Business inventory is a whole different animal that we won't tackle in this book.

As you may recall from previous chapters, Capital Gain assets are subject to Capital Gains tax rates. They are usually lower than ordinary income tax rates and come with more favorable charitable deductions too. When you donate a long term capital asset to charity, your deduction is typically based on the asset's fair market value on the date it is given. If it's a short term capital asset, the deduction is limited to basis. Ordinary income assets don't receive this same treatment. Their charitable deduction is typically the *lesser of cost basis or fair market value.*

"Basis" is a very important term. We've gone through it in previous chapters, but let's go over it again for good measure. Basis is generally the amount you paid for something or what you've invested in it. It can be more or less than what you paid for it, but that's the simple explanation. If you sell an appreciated capital asset, you recognize capital gains tax on the difference between your basis and the sale price. When you donate a long term capital asset to charity, you get to avoid that capital gains tax AND receive a deduction based on the fair market value. That's a nice double benefit that doesn't come with non-capital assets.

When it comes to Tangible Property, you'll want to know about the *Related Use Rule.* This rule incentivizes donors to contribute Tangible Property to a charity that will use the asset for something related to its mission, rather than just sell it. If a donor contributes Tangible Property to a charity that will use it for something *related* to its charitable mission, her charitable deduction is based on the fair market value. If she donates it to a charity that will sell the asset, the deduction is limited to the donor's *basis.*

Here's a good example to illustrate how this works. If a donor contributes a sculpture to an art museum and the museum will display it or use it in some other way related to their mission, the donor's charitable income tax deduction is based on the fair market value. If that same donor contributes the same sculpture to a food shelf and the food shelf sells it, the donor's charitable income tax deduction is limited to her basis.

Additionally, if the asset is unrelated to the charity's mission, the donor is not allowed to carry forward any unused portion of the deduction to future tax years. Nearly all other charitable contributions can be deducted over six years (gift year + 5) if the donor doesn't have enough income to use it against. Unrelated gifts of Tangible Property are not afforded that additional time.

Now, I hate to break it to you, but there is an exception to the *Related Use Rule* for creators of Tangible Property. If someone creates a piece of tangible property (such as a painting) and donates it to a charity that will use it for their mission, the creator's charitable income tax deduction is limited to their basis. That's going to be pretty low—probably just the cost of the canvas, paints, frame, etc.

Just as with all non-cash assets, if the donor wishes to take a charitable income tax deduction for her gift of Tangible Property, she will need to acquire a *Qualified Appraisal* of the asset and file it along with IRS Form 8283 with her tax return. The charity will need to sign the Form 8283, but should NOT complete it for the donor. Further, the charity should sign only *after* it's been completed and signed by the appraiser. For more information *Qualified Appraisals,* see IRS Publications 526 or 561.

Vehicles

Vehicles are Tangible Property, but they come with some special tax rules. If the vehicle is donated to a charity that will use it for something *related to* its charitable mission, the charitable income tax deduction is the fair market value of the vehicle. If donated to a charity that is going to sell the vehicle, rather than use it, the deduction is the *lesser of* fair market value or the sales proceeds the charity receives for the vehicle.

Donated boats will require a *Qualified Appraisal* and are still subject to the *Related Use Rule*.

STEP 2: ASK FOR THE RIGHT INFORMATION

When someone offers to contribute tangible property to your charity, you'll want to collect some important information. You'll certainly want to know *what* the donor wants to contribute and *how much* it may be worth. That way, you'll know if it meets with your gift acceptance policies. You'll want to know how the donor acquired the item as well. *Provenance* is very important. If a donor can't prove they acquired the item in a legitimate way (purchase, inheritance, etc.) and that the piece is authentic, you may want to decline the gift. If you do accept it without good provenance, you'll probably have a tough time selling it. Auctioneers and buyers are wary of purchasing items without authenticated provenance.

I also recommend viewing the item so you can assess the general condition. If you're far away and can't get to the item easily, a video call or digital photographs can be helpful. At the end of this chapter, you'll find a sample *Tangible Property Questionnaire*. It is a sample and meant to get you started. You will want to edit it to meet your organization's needs.

STEP 3: EVALUATE FOR OPPORTUNITY AND RISK

Tangible Property can be worth a fortune, so it can bring enormous opportunity for your organization. It can also be worth very little on the open market and be more of a nuisance than a gift. It may require some investigation to determine which it is.

One of the most important concerns you'll have is how quickly you can sell the item. Sales are most often handled by auctioneers, such as Christie's or Sotheby's. There are others, but these are some names you may have heard of. They can be quite helpful in determining whether there is a market for sale.

Vehicles

A vehicle donation program is a considerable undertaking, because vehicles are large, subject to licensing, and need to be transported, housed, and protected. When accepting a vehicle, you'll want to consider things like transfer of title, transfer of license plates, and insurance. Most charities that operate vehicle donation programs hire an agency to handle it for them. I think that is a wonderful idea, because it can be laborious. What charity wants to deal with collecting, storing, and selling vehicles? You have better things to do with your valuable time. Get a professional to handle it if you're going to accept vehicles.

STEP 4: ACCEPT OR DECLINE RESPECTFULLY

Acceptance

Tangible Property is transferred by *Deed of Gift*. At the end of this chapter, you'll find a sample *Deed of Gift* form for Tangible Property. It is a sample and intended to get you started. You'll want to have it reviewed by your legal counsel to make sure it meets legal requirements in your state. Your donor or her advisors may wish to edit it or use their own form.

Let the donor know what you will do with the gift once it's received. It's important to be transparent with donors. If your gift acceptance policies require you to sell immediately and reinvest into a board-approved investment portfolio, make sure you say so. Whatever your intent, let the donor know what will happen to their gift after receipt.

When accepting any non-cash asset, make sure your Gift Acknowledgment does NOT list a value for the gift. Simply describe the donated property in specific terms.

Tangible Property can be intricate and complex. I recommend you consult experienced legal counsel to make sure your description is accurate.

In addition to special tax rules, vehicle donations require special language on the gift acknowledgment. I recommend you consult IRS Publication 4302 to understand those special requirements.

Declining Respectfully

If after you complete your due diligence, you determine that the gift is unacceptable for whatever reason—you'll need to decline respectfully.

The donor has offered a generous gift and it is important to acknowledge that. I recommend meeting with the donor to 1) thank them for their offer, and 2) explain *exactly why* you are unable to accept their gift. Explain in clear terms and illustrate your reasons. I also recommend explaining your decision in writing and giving it to the donor so they can refer back to it later or share with her advisors.

If the donor really cares for your organization, she will understand why you must decline. She may even consider donating a different asset that brings you less risk.

STEP 5: MANAGE OR LIQUIDATE

If you choose to retain the Tangible Property for any period of time or to keep it indefinitely, you'll want to consider safe storage. Large, delicate, or highly valuable items can be tricky to store. In addition, you'll want to consider purchasing appropriate insurance for the item for whatever time you hold it—whether it's a week or for generations.

Recently, I toured a very unique facility in a major metropolitan area. They specialize in storing art and antiques for people who don't have a good, safe place to keep them. The facility I visited had made special accommodations to control humidity, temperature, light, insect infestation, and other conditions that could damage art and antiques. This kind of facility can be particularly useful for a charity that wishes to accept delicate and/or valuable tangible property and keep it safe until they are able to display or sell it. It is a unique place, but I expect more to pop up in other metropolitan areas.

Liquidation is typically handled by an auction house. They may be willing to transport and store the item for you for a short time prior to the sale. If you do hire an auctioneer, you'll likely need to sign an auction contract that includes a commission/buyer's premium to be paid to the auctioneer. Sometimes that's paid by the seller and sometimes by the buyer. Make sure you understand all the terms of the contract before signing. Don't be afraid to ask questions. You probably don't deal in selling things like fine art and collectibles regularly, so don't feel like you have to know everything about how it's done. That's what professionals are for—to help walk you through it and understand every step.

Vehicles

When it comes to handling and liquidating vehicles, you'll want to review IRS Publication 4302—*A Charity's Guide to Vehicle Donation*—to make sure you're up to date on all the necessary rules and regulations. You may also want to check out IRS Publication 4303—*A Donor's Guide to Vehicle Donation*—to fully understand the donor's side of the contribution.

If Tangible Property assets are sold within 3 years of the gift, the charity must file IRS Form 8282 with the IRS. This form lets the IRS know how much the assets were sold for. The IRS matches the 8282 with the 8283 filed by the donor to compare the deduction the donor took with the ultimate sale price of the gift. If the assets were sold for substantially less than the deduction value claimed by the donor, it is likely the donor could face an audit of that gift. That is one reason the charity should try to get the highest and best value when selling the assets. **They should not feel compelled to sell to anyone for a discounted price or at unreasonably favorable terms.** An audit by the IRS could view this as "private benefit" on the part of the charity and the company. *Private benefit* can come with stiff financial penalties (25% excise tax, for example) for the company, the donor, the charity, employees, and board members of the charity who were involved in the transaction. The charity's nonprofit status can also be revoked in serious cases of private benefit.

SPECIAL CONSIDERATIONS FOR GIFTS OF TANGIBLE PROPERTY TO FUND CHARITABLE GIFT ANNUITIES OR CHARITABLE REMAINDER TRUSTS

Charitable Gift Annuities:

Accepting a gift of Tangible Property or a Vehicle in exchange for a Charitable Gift Annuity (CGA) can be a risky business. When a charity enters into a CGA agreement with a donor, it is agreeing to make fixed payments to the annuitant(s) for life. The payment obligation is a general debt of the charity. As long as the charity has assets, the payments must be made. If the charity accepts an asset to fund an immediate CGA and it takes some time to sell, the charity must dip into its own reserves to make those payments. Furthermore, gift annuity payments are based upon the value of the property when it is donated, regardless of how much it sells for. If it sells for less than the value at the time of the gift, the charity will still have to make payments based on that higher amount.

Here's an example:

Tangible Property value at time of gift: $350,000
ACGA immediate CGA rate for the income beneficiary 6%
Annual Payments: $350,000 x 6% = **$21,000**

Net Sales Proceeds: $300,000
$300,000 x 6% = $18,000
Charity makes up difference of $3,000/year

If the donor lives another 20 years, that's a difference of **$60,000 the charity must cover from their own reserves.**

It is possible to accept illiquid assets like Tangible Property or a Vehicle in exchange for a CGA, but you should be aware of the risks when you are creating your policies.

Some charities attempt to mitigate these risks by offering a rate slightly lower than the standard ACGA[27] rate. Additionally, some only issue *deferred* gift annuity agreements in exchange for illiquid assets. That allows the charity time to sell the asset before they have to begin making payments.

You'll have to decide for yourself whether you're willing to accept Tangible Property to fund a gift annuity. If you ultimately decide it is too risky, you could seek out another provider who is willing to issue the gift annuity and then pass all or a majority of the residuum to your organization at the end of the CGA.

It's best to explore all options ahead of time so that you are prepared when someone inquires about donating an illiquid asset in exchange for a CGA. You don't want to have to figure out your options in the moment. Create your own policies and partner with another provider to facilitate gifts that carry more risk than you are comfortable carrying yourself.

Another option is to talk to the donor about using the asset to fund a Charitable Remainder Trust instead. That solution takes virtually all the risk off the charity. They aren't on the hook to make payments, invest the sales proceeds, or perform administration. The trustee of the CRT is responsible for all of that.

The main concerns from the charity's perspective are:
  A. The donor can retain the ability to change the charitable beneficiaries in the CRT agreement; and
  B. The donor may likely name more than one charitable beneficiary and that could lessen your ultimate share of the gift.

These aren't significant risks and are significantly offset by eliminating all the risks associated with accepting asset to fund a CGA yourself.

Charitable Remainder Unitrust
In general, Tangible Property or a very valuable Vehicle can be ideal gifts to donate to a CRT. The CRT trustee sells the property tax-free—leaving 100% of the net sales proceeds available to reinvest and make the trust payments to the trust beneficiary(ies). When the CRT comes to its scheduled end, the remaining assets are distributed to the charities the donor named in the trust agreement.

It is a best practice to utilize the *Flip Charitable Remainder Unitrust* for gifts of any illiquid asset. The *Flip* feature gives the trustee time to market and sell the property before making payments to the income beneficiaries. The *Unitrust* feature protects the trust from erosion due to potential volatility in the sales price of the property or fluctuation in the value of trust investments over time. The payments from a *Unitrust* are based on the

---

27 America Council on Gift Annuities

value of the trust assets and the payment calculation is re-established every year. For example, if the *Unitrust* payment percentage is 6% and the trust asset value in year one is $100,000, the payment in that year would be $6,000.

$$\$100,000 \times 6\% = \$6,000$$

If the trust asset value is $110,000 in year two, the payment that year would be $6,600.

$$\$110,000 \times 6\% = \$6,600$$

Notice the payout percentage does not change. That is constant and is written into the trust document. The payments will fluctuate every year depending on how the trust assets are invested. This provides some protection for the remainder value to charity.

A Charitable Remainder Annuity Trust (CRAT) is not recommended for gifts of illiquid assets. If it were used, the payout would be based on the payout percentage and the value of the gift on the date of the gift. If the property sells for less than the gift value and the investments perform poorly, the trust could be significantly depleted leaving little to nothing for charity at the end. Furthermore, the *Flip* feature cannot be added to a CRAT. Without that feature, the trustee would have to make payments immediately, regardless of whether the property had sold or not. If the property hasn't sold and the trust has no liquid assets, the only way to make a payment would be to deed shares of the property to the income recipient. That creates a whole host of problems that we won't go into here. Just know that when dealing with gifts of illiquid assets, the *FLIP CRUT* is the trust type of choice.

One risk of note is when charities serve as the *trustee* of a Charitable Remainder Trust. Some charities do this as a matter of practice, but you should be aware of the risks. A trustee is responsible for many things, including:

- Asset management and investment
- Annual tax filings
- Payments to human income beneficiaries
- Protecting assets for the human and charitable beneficiaries

Litigation is not uncommon. The human or charitable beneficiaries may feel the trustee has mismanaged the assets or misreported data on the tax filings and could file a lawsuit. Furthermore, these are *tax-exempt* trusts. The IRS keeps a very close eye on them.

A trustee is considered a *fiduciary*. Fiduciaries have a *legal* duty to protect the interests of those they are charged with protecting. In this case, it's the human and charitable beneficiaries. Violation of that duty could result in severe penalties for the trustee as an organization or for the individual at the organization who is in charge of managing the trust.

Think twice before agreeing to serve as trustee of a Charitable Remainder Trust. Understand all the risks and get professional legal guidance before you do it.

Sample Tangible Property Gift Procedures

1. Conduct initial conversations with donor about gift basics.

2. Donor completes and returns the *Tangible Property Questionnaire.*

3. Review *Tangible Property Questionnaire* and any accompanying documentation. If no red flags exist, begin asset transfer. If red flags do exist, work with donor to clarify or fix before moving forward.

4. Discuss with donor the method of sale: auction, private sale to interested buyers, broker, etc. It is a best practice to consult with a reputable auction house to inquire about marketability before the gift is accepted.

5. Title is transferred via *Deed of Gift*. Provide donor with *Tangible Property Deed of Gift* form to review with her advisors, complete, and sign. Donor's advisors may wish to use a different form or edit the form.

6. Once asset transfers, liquidation can begin in the method charity feels best.

7. Sales proceeds transferred to charity.

8. Charity sends donor a written acknowledgment of the gift.

Sample Tangible Property Gift Questionnaire

1. What type of property would you like to donate?

    _____

    _____

    _____

2. How did you acquire the property?

    _____

    _____

    _____

3. Do you have any written documentation of ownership?   YES   NO
    If yes, please attach a copy.

4. What is the approximate value of the property you wish to donate? Please list
    items separately.

    _____

    _____

    _____

5. Is the property insured?   YES   NO
    If yes, please attach a copy of the policy.

6. Please attach at least one photograph of the property you wish to donate.

Please contact us right away with any questions or concerns you have about this questionnaire. We want you to be absolutely comfortable with your proposed gift. We also want to create an open conversation with you and your advisors about why this information is needed and how it will be used.

I understand that the truth and accuracy of my answers to the previous questions will be relied upon when evaluating my proposed gift of tangible property. I certify that each of the answers is true, accurate, and complete to the best of my knowledge.

_____   _____

Signature   Date

_____   _____

Print name   Phone Number

Sample Deed of Gift Tangible Personal Property

With no consideration, I _____hereby irrevocably give and transfer to _____, all rights, title and interest, including physical possession, in and to the following tangible personal property:

_____

_____

_____

_____

_____

_____

On this _____ day of _____, 20_____ in the County of _____, State of _____, I hereby sign this Deed of Gift of Tangible Personal Property.

_____

Signature

State of _____

County of _____

Signed or attested before me on _____, by

_____

(Seal, if any)

_____

Signature of notarial officer   Title

My commission expires: _____

Chapter 9:
Gifts of Intangible Property

Intangible property can be a confusing asset type, because you can't see it or touch it. It exists "on paper" or electronically. The most common types you'll run into are *Virtual Currency, Intellectual Property,* and *Mineral Interests.*

We will cover each of these three types individually within each of step of our *5-Step process.*

1. **Know the Basics**
2. **Ask for the Right Information**
3. **Evaluate for Opportunity and Risk**
4. **Accept or Decline Respectfully**
5. **Manager or Liquidate**

STEP 1: KNOW THE BASICS

Virtual Currency

Many charities today are debating whether to accept virtual currency (VC). You may even wonder "is it even real?" Even some of our most respected financial minds are skeptical of it and refuse to take part. Whatever your personal feelings, it is a real thing; it can be extremely valuable, and people are legitimately giving it to charity.

Virtual currencies are not issued by a government entity and are not regulated like the monies we are most familiar with—the US Dollar, British Pound, Japanese Yen, etc. Virtual currencies exist in electronic form only. Like many people, I was initially very skeptical of VC and assumed it would eventually just dry up and blow away like most fads. Then, I started learning more and it started to make sense.

Imagine you live in a country with an unstable government and currency. You're trying to purchase goods from other countries or operate a business. It can be difficult if your currency fluctuates wildly in value every day or inflation is out of control. You may wish to "opt-out" of your country's currency and use a more "global" currency that isn't subject to the whims of your unstable government. That's where something like virtual currency might make sense. In fact, many people who live in volatile nations are using virtual currency regularly to buy and sell goods. They do so by using simple apps on their smartphones. There are many other reasons that virtual currency might make sense for someone, but this is one of the most compelling situations that I've encountered.

The term *Virtual Currency* includes many different types of electronic currency, including *Cryptocurrency*. Cryptocurrency uses cryptography to create more secure transactions, and that's the kind you're most likely to encounter.

Even though we describe VC as "currency", the IRS says it's not. For tax purposes, virtual currency is considered personal property. This is important, because it determines how VC transactions are taxed and valued.

If you acquired virtual currency by purchase or through "mining", it is considered a *capital asset* and is subject to capital gains tax rates. If you acquired it as payment for services (like wages), it is considered ordinary income property and subject to ordinary income tax rates.

As you may recall from earlier chapters, long term *Capital Assets* are deductible at their fair market value when donated to charity, and *Ordinary Income Assets* are usually deductible at the *lesser of cost basis or fair market value*. This means that if you donate VC to charity, your deduction is going to depend upon how you acquired it.

Virtual Currency is traded on exchanges. There are thousands of them around the world. They are sort of like the New York Stock Exchange, but they are not a physical place. They exist electronically. If you donate publicly traded stock, which is traded on a *physical* exchange, the value of your deduction is based on the daily trading price of that stock.

The IRS does not recognize virtual exchanges for purposes of valuing donations of virtual currency. That means that donations of VC must be valued by *Qualified Appraisal*. Qualified appraisals require specific elements and methodology. There are very few companies that provide Qualified appraisals for donations of virtual currency. The one that I'm most familiar with is *Charitable Solutions, LLC*. They perform quite a few of them and use a repeatable methodology. If a donor wants to take a charitable deduction for their gift of virtual currency, they will have to get a Qualified appraisal and submit it along with IRS Form 8283 signed by the charity and the appraiser.

 *Charities should NOT complete Form 8283 for a donor, and they should only sign it once it has been completed and signed by both the donor and the appraiser.*

If you want to accept virtual currency, you'll need to set up a *Digital Wallet* with a processor firm, such as *BitPay*. A digital wallet is kind of like a brokerage account you might establish for accepting gifts of stock. These processor firms accept certain types of VC and will convert it to US dollars for you. Establishing a digital wallet for a charity can be an enormous hurdle. Not all processors will work with charities for fear of money laundering and fraud. If they are willing to work with a charity, it takes a long time to set up your wallet. The firm will likely require a LOT of personal information about the charity's executives and board members, including home addresses and Social Security numbers. They do this to prevent fraud. They want to know *exactly* who they're dealing with. Unfortunately, disclosing all this personal information is very burdensome upon charities and many decide to forgo gifts of VC entirely.

If you run into this kind of trouble, I encourage you to seek out a helper that will accept a gift of VC on your behalf. They make it easy and help you to bypass the burdens of having your own digital wallet. The two that I am most familiar with are *The Giving Block* and *Dechomai Foundation*.

Intellectual Property

Intellectual Property includes a long list of intangible property types, including things like *Copyrights, Patents, Software,* and *Trademarks.* This book won't go into great detail on each type, nor will you find procedures or questionnaires for these kinds of property at the end of the chapter. They are very complex and individually unique. I advise working closely with your outside counsel to evaluate and process a gift of Intellectual Property. That being said, I will go through some basics that will help you in the initial stages of a gift discussion with a donor.

Intellectual Property is generally considered an ordinary income asset and thus the charitable deduction is the *lesser of cost basis or fair market value.* In some cases, it is more financially beneficial for a donor to sell the Intellectual Property and donate cash to receive a larger charitable deduction. If a donor *does* contribute the Intellectual Property to charity, they may be able to deduct the income the charity receives from it over time. (Think royalties from a patent or copyright.) This requires *significant* reporting and assumes the charity retains the Intellectual Property, rather than selling it.

Gifts of Intellectual Property require a *Qualified Appraisal* and an IRS Form 8283 signed by the charity and appraiser.

Mineral Interests

About 5-10 years ago, gifts of mineral interests to charity were a hot topic. They still happen, but they aren't as much in the news. Mineral interests come from different natural resources, such as *oil, gas, coal,* and *precious metals.* The interests can be donated as *Leases, Royalties,* or *Working Interests.*

If the minerals are still in the ground, the donor may or may not be able to contribute the interests to charity. Some states allow bifurcation of real estate from mineral interests. Some do not. If not, they are tied to the real estate and can only be donated along with the "surface" real estate.

A donation of mineral interests will require a Qualified Appraisal and IRS Form 8283 if the donor wishes to take a charitable deduction. These appraisals can be very expensive because they require specific expertise of people like geologists and engineers. The appraisal must also consider both the current and potential future yields of the excavation.

STEP 2: ASK FOR THE RIGHT INFORMATION

Virtual Currency

The first thing you'll want to know is what kind of VC the donor wishes to contribute. Your digital wallet will likely only accept certain types. If the donor wishes to donate one outside your capabilities, I advise consulting with one of the helpers I described above to see if they might be able to accept on your behalf.

Next, you'll want to know the approximate value to make sure it meets your gift minimums.

It is a VERY good practice to make sure you really *know* the donor. You don't want to get into a situation where someone acquired virtual currency through nefarious means and is now looking to "launder" it by making a charitable gift. VC is often used as a payment method in the criminal underworld. You don't want to be a part of that. If a stranger approaches your organization offering to donate virtual currency, do your homework and make sure you know as much as you can about this person before you decide to accept a gift—no matter how big it is.

At the end of this chapter, you'll find a questionnaire you can use to collect basic information about the VC, not the donor. I don't recommend requesting personal information about a donor in a paper questionnaire. Personal information should always be collected in a secure format to prevent it being stolen.

Intellectual Property and Mineral Interests

These are very broad asset types with countless nuances and variety. For that reason, I'm not going to go into great detail as to what information to gather. Instead, I recommend you find out:

A. The *type* of property (*patent, copyright, royalty, etc.*)
B. The *approximate value* of the property
C. *How* the donor acquired the property

Once you have these pieces of information, I recommend working closely with experienced legal counsel to develop a plan to evaluate the gift.

STEP 3: EVALUATE FOR OPPORTUNITY AND RISK

Virtual Currency

Once you have established a solid framework for accepting and liquidating virtual currency, the opportunities are significant and the risks minimal. Your current and potential donors own very valuable quantities of virtual currency. If you can make it simple for them to donate it, you'll both benefit greatly.

The main risk with accepting virtual currency is quick liquidation. The value does fluctuate widely, so you've got to be ready to liquidate it almost immediately upon receipt.

Generally, there are still concerns about virtual currency being used to fund criminal activity, but these concerns are becoming less and less as more security measures are put into place to verify transactions.

If your organization feels uneasy about accepting virtual currency, do not give up. I strongly encourage you to partner with one of the helpers I mentioned above. They are happy to accept VC on your behalf.

Intellectual Property

Intellectual Property can be extremely valuable and bring significant opportunities to your organization. That being said, it may be difficult to liquidate. You probably don't want to hold onto it for any longer than you absolutely have to. Like any asset, you'll need to value it each year to report on your Form 990, and it can be a cumbersome process to get a valuation. If you do hold onto it, it may bring the risk of Unrelated Business Taxable Income (UBTI). That's usually only if the income from it comprises a significant portion of your income. The due diligence, management, and liquidation can require a great deal of time and expense. You'll have to decide if you want to handle it yourself or farm out to a helper organization to accept on your behalf.

Mineral Interests

There are a variety of types of mineral interests, and most of them won't bring significant risks to a charity owner because the charity is a "passive" investor. The charity owns the mineral interests much as they would stock in a public company. If a charity accepts a *working interest* in minerals, that can bring UBTI and potentially legal and financial liability. For that reason, I highly recommend that charities think twice before accepting a working interest in a mining venture. If you consider it, make sure to get the very best legal and tax advice before proceeding.

As with all non-cash assets, a big concern is ease of liquidation. What is your exit plan? There is generally a ready market for the sale of all kinds of mineral interests, so you probably won't have trouble selling them to a buyer at a good price.

STEP 4: ACCEPT OR DECLINE RESPECTFULLY

Acceptance
Virtual currency is transferred electronically similarly to the electronic transfer of stock. Intellectual Property and Mineral Interests are transferred by *Deed of Gift*.

Let the donor know what you will do with the gift once it's received. It's important to be transparent with donors. If your gift acceptance policies require you to sell immediately and reinvest into a board-approved investment portfolio, make sure you say so. Whatever your intent, let the donor know what will happen to their gift after receipt.

When accepting any non-cash asset, make sure your Gift Acknowledgment does NOT list a value for the gift. Simply describe the donated property in specific terms.

Virtual currency can be described by number of units. Intellectual Property and Mineral Interests are more complex, and you'll want to consult experienced legal counsel to make sure your description is accurate.

Declining Respectfully
If after you complete your due diligence, you determine that the gift is unacceptable for whatever reason, you'll need to decline respectfully.

The donor has offered a generous gift and it is important to acknowledge that. I recommend meeting with the donor to 1) thank them for their offer, and 2) explain *exactly why* you are unable to accept their gift. Explain in clear terms and illustrate your reasons. I also recommend explaining your decision in writing and giving it to the donor so she can refer back to it later and share with her advisors.

If the donor really cares for your organization, she should understand why you must decline. They may decide to consider donating a different asset that brings you less risk.

STEP 5: MANAGE OR LIQUIDATE

The vast majority of charities will sell intangible property, rather than hold and manage it. There will be certain situations when you will want to hold onto it, but in most cases, liquidation will be the preferred course of action. You'll want to put those sales proceeds to work on your mission as soon as possible.

Virtual currency can be liquidated very quickly on an online exchange. Intellectual property will take a bit more time and probably require the assistance of a broker and intellectual property attorney to find and negotiate with appropriate buyers. Sales contracts should always be in writing, and you should know as much as possible about the buyer before you sell.

Mineral interests are typically easy to sell because there are thousands of interested buyers at any given time. You may want to hire a broker to help you maximize the number of potential buyers, save you time, and make sure all the details are handled in a professional manner.

If you sell any Intangible Property within three years of the gift date, you'll need to file Form 8282 with the IRS. This form simply states how much you sold the property for. The IRS matches this up with the Form 8283 the donor filed to substantiate her charitable income tax deduction to make sure the deduction was in line with the ultimate sale price of the asset. If the sale price is significantly *lower* than the deducted value, the donor could quite possibly be audited. Large and potentially fraudulent charitable income tax deductions are one of the most commonly audited transactions. For that reason, I recommend that charities try their very best to get the highest and best sale price for any non-cash donation.

Sample **Virtual Currency Gift Procedures**

1. Conduct initial conversations with donor about gift basics.

2. Donor completes and returns the *Virtual Currency Gift Questionnaire.*

3. Review completed *Virtual Currency Gift Questionnaire.*

4. If any red flags arise from review of *Virtual Currency Gift Questionnaire,* resolve, if possible.

5. If no red flags exist and gift meets the minimum, work with donor to execute transfer of ownership to charity's digital wallet.

6. Liquidate virtual currency as soon as possible upon receipt.

7. Send donor a written acknowledgment of the gift.

Sample Virtual Currency Gift Questionnaire

Please answer the following questions to the best of your ability. Accuracy and thoroughness are vital to the proper care of your gift. Any information you share will be held in the strictest of confidence and only shared with necessary staff, legal, and tax counsel.

1. What type of virtual currency would you like to donate?

_____

2. How many shares/units would you like to donate?

_____

3. What is the estimated value per share/unit?

_____

4. How did you acquire the virtual currency?

____ Mining

____ Compensation

____ Purchase

____ Other (Please explain)

_____

Please contact us right away with any questions or concerns you have about this questionnaire. We want you to be absolutely comfortable with your proposed gift. We also want to create an open conversation with you and your advisors about why this information is needed and how it will be used.

I understand that the truth and accuracy of my answers to the previous questions will be relied upon when evaluating my proposed gift of virtual currency. I certify that each of the answers is true, accurate, and complete to the best of my knowledge.

_____   _____
Signature   Date

_____   _____
Print name   Phone Number

Chapter 10:
Donor Advised Funds

This book would be incomplete without a thorough discussion of Donor Advised Funds. No matter your personal feelings about DAFs, they are powerful tools. They are perfectly designed to turn non-cash assets into exceptional charitable gifts.

This chapter will walk you through:
- *HOW* Donor Advised Funds work,
- The 3 basic TYPES you'll encounter,
- *WHY* they've become so powerful, and
- *HOW* an operating charity can use them to their advantage.

Before we dive in, let's set the stage by taking a look at the DAF landscape in America. Every year, more and more people establish their own Donor Advised Funds and virtually all measurements of DAFs increase. Even during the Great Recession, DAF numbers rose.[28] Each year, contributions into DAFs increase and grants out increase. The only number that has been consistently falling is the average size of a Donor Advised Fund. That's because more people of relatively modest means are establishing them. They're not just for the very wealthy anymore.

People are using DAFs as a tool to centralize and streamline their giving. **They're also using them as a way to contribute large, non-cash assets and have the sales proceeds of those assets distributed to multiple charities.** That's why we're looking at DAFs—for their power to *Turn Wealth Into What Matters*.

---

[28] *National Philanthropic Trust: 2021 Donor Advised Fund Study; www.nptrust.org*

HOW DONOR ADVISED FUNDS WORK

Donor Advised Funds are offered by three primary sources:
- Community Foundations
- National Providers (Fidelity Charitable, Schwab Charitable, etc.), and
- Single-Issue Charities, such as universities and hospitals.

All donor advised funds work on the same principle.
1. Donors create a fund with a DAF provider. This is typically memorialized in something called a "Fund Agreement", which outlines how the fund will operate.
2. Donors contribute assets to their fund.
3. In return, they receive the same charitable income tax deduction they would for making that gift to any other public charity.
4. The provider sells any non-cash gifts and reinvests the proceeds into a diversified portfolio.
5. Donors request grants from their fund to their favorite charities.
6. The DAF provider liquidates some of the investments in the fund to make cash available for the grant and sends a check to the charity.

That's it. They ALL work that way. **The primary difference is how *quickly* or *slowly* donors request grants from their funds.** Some donors like what I call the "fast and furious" approach. They want as much to go out to operating charities as fast as possible. Others prefer the "slow and steady" approach. They like the idea of the fund being a permanent source of income for their favorite charities—sort of like an endowment. And still other donors fall somewhere in between.

Currently, there is no Federal or State regulation mandating a certain payout percentage from DAFs. There have been bills introduced at both the Federal and State levels that, if passed, would require a certain minimum payout from DAF providers. Proponents of these mandates feel that DAFs should be held to the same standard as Private Foundations when it comes to mandatory distributions. Private Foundations are required by federal law to distribute at least 5% of their total value to charity every year, and that's about what they distribute. According to research conducted by National Philanthropic Trust, DAFs—on average—distribute more than 20% of their value annually.

Opponents to mandatory distribution feel that DAFs already distribute more than the proposed mandates, so why mess with something that's operating just fine on its own. The debates are ongoing. I encourage you to read both sides of the discussion and make up your own mind.

Contributions *into* a Donor Advised Fund are charitable gifts to a public charity. All DAF providers are public charities. That's why the donor receives an income tax deduction when they make a gift into the fund. When the gift is made, the donor gives up legal ownership and control of the donated assets. They retain "advisory" capabilities. That means they can *request* grants be distributed to the charities they choose. The provider has the legal right to decline that grant based on their own internal policies and the law. That right is called their *variance power*. It's very important that they have this power. It's what allows donors to receive charitable deductions when they make contributions to their funds. The DAF provider must have ultimate control over the assets in the fund.

This is a good place to pause and dispel a common myth about DAFs. **DAF providers do NOT tell donors where they can and can't make grants.** They DO prevent donors from making grants to fake charities and charities that have lost their charitable status with the IRS. They do this because it is *illegal* for them to make such grants. DAF providers are required by law to only send grants to legitimate public charities. They are also not allowed to send grants to Private Foundations. That's because the income tax deductions for private foundations are more restrictive than to public charities. To make a grant from a DAF to a private foundation would be skirting those rules. Many providers also disallow grants to charities that have been deemed "hate groups".

Some "single-issue" charities that offer DAFs sometimes implement additional policies that prevent grants to organizations with missions counter to their own. Single-issue charities are organizations with their own charitable mission, such as universities, hospitals, religious institutions, etc. More and more of them are offering DAFs these days. You can imagine why a single-issue charity may decline a grant request to a charity doing work counter to their own beliefs and mission.

DAFs COME IN THREE BASIC "FLAVORS"

Every DAF provider offers a few different varieties of funds to meet donor preferences. They each call them something different, so I want to outline each variety, so you'll be able to recognize them when you see them - no matter what they're called.

I use the following terms to describe them:
1. **Flexible**
2. **Auto-Pilot**
3. **Mission-Based**

The "Flexible" DAF

This style is the one you're probably most familiar with. It's the *original* flavor, if you will.

- Donors make contributions into the fund when they want to.
- They request grants out of the fund to their favorite charities when they want to.

They can choose a different charity every time or stick with the same ones. It's up to them. They can request whatever grant amount suits them—as long as it meets the provider's minimum grant amount. Grant minimums are usually $250 or less.

It's a very simple, fluid, and flexible approach. Many providers have eliminated their minimum balance requirement or have reduced minimums considerably. Donors are free to request all or nearly all of their DAF balance to be granted out to their favorite charities.

The "Auto-Pilot" DAF

This is the *slow and steady* style.

- Donors make contributions to the fund when they want to.
- At the time the fund is established, the donor chooses a list of charities to receive grants each year going forward.
- Sometimes these funds are established during the donor's lifetime but not funded until after they've passed away. The fund sits empty waiting for a future contribution.
- Once a contribution has been made to the fund, grants are automatically sent to the list of charities the donor has created.

Distributions tend to be annual and are usually a percentage of the fund's total value. Annual distributions are usually around 5%. A moderate distribution amount like this allows the fund to retain a pretty stable balance over time and hopefully grow slowly. That way, the recipient charities can rely on a steady stream of grants each year for a very long time—sometimes generations or even into perpetuity.

Distributions percentages can be higher if the donor wishes the fund to deplete over a period of time, rather than operate in perpetuity.

Some providers will allow the donor to change their list of charities. Some do not.

The "Mission-Based" DAF

The type allows the donor to create a "mission statement" for their fund. The mission tends to focus on one area of charitable work but doesn't restrict grants to a set list of charities. Each year the DAF provider goes out and searches for charities doing work that matches the fund's mission statement. They send out requests for proposals (RFPs) to those charities and award the annual grant to the charity(ies) that best fulfills the fund's purpose.

These funds aren't as common as the first two. They appeal to a smaller segment of donors, and they require a higher contribution to start and maintain. As you can imagine, this type of fund requires more work on the part of the provider's staff and the grants need to be large enough to make it worth the charities' while to submit a detailed proposal.

This type usually distributes a percentage of its annual value. A common distribution percentage is 5%, which allows the fund to maintain its value, grow slowly over time, and ensure a nice grant amount each year.

Blended Varieties

Sometimes providers will allow donors to "blend" these three varieties. For example, a fund may start out as *flexible* during the donor's lifetime. After they pass away, the fund converts to *auto-pilot* or *mission-based* because the donor is no longer alive to request grants.

Sometimes providers will allow donors to convert their fund from one type to another during their lifetime. They may start out with one variety but realize they'd rather have another type. Ultimately, the provider wants the donor to have a positive experience, so they will allow the donor to make these kinds of changes.

Now, no matter what label a provider puts on a type of DAF, you'll be able to recognize it as one of these three types and understand how it works.

FEATURES

Different providers offer different features to meet donor needs. I think of them like toppings on a pizza. Every pizza has the same basic foundation—crust and sauce (and most of the time cheese). Then, you pick your toppings. DAFs are the same. They have the same basic foundation we outlined above and then the donor picks her features or "toppings".

Not all DAFs come with the same features. **When choosing a provider, it's RE-ALLY important to think about how you want your fund to work and how you want to use it.** Donors should choose a provider that offers features that match the vision they have for your fund. Many people consider management fees only when choosing a provider. They don't consider all the other features and end up with a less than ideal experience.

Let's look at some of the more significant features that people consider when choosing a Donor Advised Fund provider.

Multi-generational

Most providers allow donors to name "successor advisors" for their fund to take over the advisory role at some point in the future (usually the donor's passing). They can name children, grandchildren, or friends to take over. Donors like this feature because it offers a sense of permanence to the fund and they can use it as a tool to pass along their values to younger generations.

Some providers allow for unlimited successor advisors. Some allow only one generational transfer. After the last advisor generation passes away, the fund will usually continue as an *auto-pilot* or *mission-based* fund.

Anonymity

This is a VERY popular feature for donors. Many people want to make gifts to their fund, get their tax deductions, and request grants to their favorite charities. They don't; however, enjoy recognition or want to risk having their names shared with other charities who add them to their mailing lists. So, they want to request grants from their fund to be sent anonymously.

Some providers will allow donors to be anonymous to some grantee charities and disclose their name to others. Some will allow the donor to be anonymous during life but disclose their name after they've passed (in the case of *auto-pilot* or *mission-based* funds).

Anonymity can be very frustrating for charities receiving grants from a DAF. They want to thank the donor who requested the grant, but they have no idea who it came from. You can contact the DAF provider and ask the name of the fund from which the grant came, but they're not likely to disclose that information. They take donor privacy very seriously.

Fees and Investments

Fees and Investments are important considerations, but they should not be given more weight than the other features. The old saying, "you get what you pay for", tends to be true.

DAF fees usually come in two forms. First, there are administrative fees, which cover the overhead expenses for the provider. They have expenses just like any non-profit—staff, benefits, office space, etc. Second, there are investment fees.

If a provider offers personalized service, such as relationship managers, educational opportunities, community expertise, tours of charities, etc.—their administrative fees will probably be higher to accommodate those services. If a provider offers a more transactional experience, their administrative fees will tend to be lower. Some donors want a more relational experience. Others prefer a more transactional one. It's best to look at both types and choose the one that fits the donor's style. The administrative fees at community foundations and single-issue charities tend to be a little bit higher because they usually offer a more relational experience. Administrative fees for DAF providers affiliated with financial firms tend to be lower, because they usually provide a more transactional experience. They also tend to be heavily subsidized by their financial service affiliates.

Investment fees reflect the underlying expenses for the managers that run the investments. You can think of these as the overhead for the investment managers—staff, benefits, office space, etc. Lower fees usually reflect a less sophisticated investment fund, but not always.

Investment fees also include any fees or commissions to be paid when the provider purchases or sells investments. Most providers invest in "Institutional Class" funds that come with no fees/commissions to purchase into or sell out of the funds. Institutional Class investments are available only to *institutional* investors, such as nonprofits, pension funds, etc. These institutions must invest in *very* large quantities in order to be able to get these "fee-free" investments.

Every provider offers different investment options for the money sitting in a DAF. Donors will have the option to choose from various portfolios, depending on how they plan to use the fund. If they plan to request large grants over a short period of time, they will probably choose a more conservative portfolio to reduce market fluctuation. If they plan to request grants more slowly over time, they may choose a more aggressive portfolio to focus on growth over time.

The investment portfolios offered are mostly a mix of mutual funds, hedge funds, and other private placements available only to very sophisticated investors. They don't tend to be individual stocks and bonds.

Recently, providers have begun offering donors the opportunity to invest their DAF assets in things like Socially Responsible Investments, Program Related Investments, Mission-Related Investments, and Impact Investments. Entire books have been written on these creatures, so we won't go into it in great detail. What I will say is that these types of investments are designed to align personal values with investing. They are a way of doing good with money even while it's sitting in an investment. I encourage you to read more about these types of investments. They are fascinating, and DAF providers are creating some really innovative ways for donors to invest their DAF dollars in ways that make their communities better.

WHY HAVE DAFs BECOME SO POPULAR?

In 2014 there were about 250,000 individual DAFs in America. In 2020, that number grew to over 1,000,000.[29] That is monumental growth. I believe there are two reasons Donor Advised Funds have seen such rapid growth.

First, the full-force adoption of DAFs by financial firms. Companies like Fidelity, Schwab, and Vanguard have created their own charities to provide DAFs to their customers. They realized that it's a very effective way to attract new customers and to retain existing customers. When you can help people give meaning to their wealth, it creates a stronger bond. These financial firms have invested heavily in their DAF providers

---

[29] *National Philanthropic Trust: 2021 Donor-Advised Fund Report;* www.nptrust.org

and equip them with the best technology, high-class investments, and professional staff who are experts in processing non-cash gifts. As a result of their strong investment and dedication to DAFs, National Providers account for 86% of the funds in existence. Community Foundations hold 8.3% and Single-Issue Charities have just 5.6%.[30]

These national providers are challenging the traditional community foundation DAF providers to up their game when it comes to technology and investments. Many community foundations are rising to the occasion and meeting the challenge. It's not easy on their smaller budgets, but they are using top-notch technology and offering world-class investment options. Add that to their existing white-glove donor treatment and you've got a real recipe for success!

Second, their ability to accept non-cash gifts. When a donor wants to use a valuable non-cash asset to support charity, they probably want to support more than one. Donor Advised Funds make this easy. The donor can contribute the asset to their fund. The provider will liquidate it tax-free. The sales proceeds are then available to be granted to the donor's favorite charities. Trying to donate one asset to multiple charities is not a task most people want to undertake. For example, imagine a donor wants to contribute a piece of real estate to 5 different charities. They could donate a 1/5 interest to each charity. Those 5 charities would each perform their own due diligence process to determine whether they want to accept it. What if some want it, but others don't have the capacity to accept? Then they would have to agree on what to do with it. If they all want to sell, they would have to coordinate a sale with a buyer. Can you imagine coordinating this kind of situation with 4 other charities? No fun.

Furthermore, most charities are not yet equipped to accept all types of non-cash gifts. They may not have the staff or the time to do so. In that case, a DAF can make non-cash gifts accessible to virtually any charity. The donor contributes the non-cash gift to the DAF. It is sold tax-free, and the sales proceeds are available to grant to the charity that couldn't accept it on their own.

HOW CAN CHARITIES USE DAFs TO THEIR ADVANTAGE?

First off, don't spend your time trying to "get in front of" a DAF provider's donors. It's not going to happen. Think about it. If a charity came to you and asked you to convene a meeting where you came and gave your pitch to *their* donors, would you agree? No, you probably wouldn't. It's not that they don't want you to know who their donors are. It's because 99% of donors who create DAFs already know who they want to make grants to. If they want help, they will ask the provider's expert staff to help them find charities doing the best work in a certain area.

---

[30] *National Philanthropic Trust: 2021 Donor-Advised Fund Report;* www.nptrust.org

That's where you can spend some time. **Make sure that your local community foundations know who you are and what you do.** That way, when a donor does come to them and ask for help selecting a charity—they can bring your organization's name into the conversation.

There are a few pro-active things you can do that will bring you considerable success in attracting more grants from DAFs.

First, talk to your existing donors and ask if they already have a donor advised fund. If they say "yes", you should be excited. This person is obviously intentional about charitable giving AND has set aside money that can *only* be used for charitable giving. I would treat them like a donor you just discovered who has their own family foundation. It's not that different.

Additionally, ask them "would you consider requesting a grant to our organization?" They may already be giving to your organization from their fund, but in an anonymous manner. This could be the conversation that prompts them to disclose that they are behind some of those mystery DAF checks your organization has received.

You could also consider asking them if someone close to them has a donor advised fund. They may not be in a position to establish a fund themselves, but a family member may. Imagine if one of your younger donors approaches her grandmother and asks, "Grandma, would you consider requesting a grant from your fund to XYZ charity?". Do you think grandma is going to say no? Probably not. She'll be thrilled to have a conversation about giving with her grandchild and more than happy to request that grant.

Second, let people know they can request grants to your organization. In your annual appeal letters, you probably have check boxes for *Cash, Check, and Credit Card*. What if you add an additional box for *"Request Grant From My Donor Advised Fund"*. It's one more touch to remind the reader of that additional way to give.

Consider adding additional giving options on your annual appeal letters for "Gift of Stock", "Qualified Charitable Distribution from my IRA", and "Request a Grant from my Donor Advised Fund". Many donors haven't considered these ways to give and are likely to do some internet research to find out more.

Third, remember you're not the only game in town. Most donors give to more than one charity. If they want to donate a valuable non-cash asset to charity, they may very well want to use it to benefit multiple organizations. Donor Advised Funds accomplish that perfectly. They can accept the asset, liquidate it, and then send the sales proceeds to the donor's favorite charities. I advise you to start a close relationship with your local community foundations so that you understand their DAF policies. That way, when one of your donors wants to use a non-cash asset to benefit multiple charities, you can be the one to help make that happen. Introduce them to your friendly neighborhood community foundation and the concept of the Donor Advised Fund. They'll be impressed with your ingenuity and preparedness.

Community Foundations can also be wonderful helpers when it comes to *your* organization's fundraising. Many of them offer Endowment management, Charitable Gift Annuity and Charitable Trust management. Many also offer DAFs for charities! Yes, your charity can establish a fund at a community foundation to receive contributions to it directly from donors. You might consider doing this to receive non-cash gifts that you don't feel comfortable accepting yourself. You may also consider doing this to take advantage of the high-quality investments they may have access to that you don't.

Many people have little awareness of the vast service and support that their local community foundations provide for both donors and nonprofits. Explore these options. You'll be glad you did.

I hope this chapter has helped you to understand Donor Advised Funds in more detail and has given you some ideas you can use right away to begin *partnering* with DAFs for your organization's benefit.

Chapter 11:
Unleash Your Success!

Now it's time to put all your new-found knowledge to use and *Unleash Your Success!* Let's recap some of the important things you need to do to set yourself up for success with non-cash charitable gifts.

REMEMBER THE 3-STEP GIFT PLAN PROCESS

All good plans come together with the help of three specific steps: 1) Goals, 2) Tools, and 3) Techniques. Focus most of your time helping donors determine their charitable goals. What are they trying to accomplish? Next, with the help of their other advisors, work with donors to identify which asset is the right one to donate to achieve their charitable and financial goals. Last, zero in on the very best technique to use their wealth to accomplish their goals. Help them *Turn Wealth Into What Matters* to them!

COMMUNICATE NON-CASH GIVING TO YOUR AUDIENCES

Tell your audiences that they can donate their non-cash wealth to achieve their charitable goals. Tell them when you're speaking in person. Tell them in print, including on paper, in social media, on your website, and in email.

Don't fall into the trap of leading with tax benefits. Lead with the *story*! Tell stories of people who have made non-cash gifts. Focus on *WHY* they made the gift. What difference were they trying to make? WHY are they passionate about your organization? What was going on in their lives that prompted them to make that gift? Close with some financial benefits of that non-cash gift and a clear call to action.

Don't forget my favorite saying: *"Taxes don't determine the WHY of the gift, but they often determine the WHEN."*

ASSEMBLE YOUR "BENCH" OF ADVISORS

It takes a team of experts to create a good non-cash gift plan. Start interviewing CPAs, Wealth Advisors, and Estate Attorneys for your "bench". Remember, these are people with special expertise who can advise both your donors and your organization.

Many donors don't have advisors who can give wealth, tax, or legal advice. Charities shouldn't be giving this kind of advice, so make sure you have a great group of advisors to whom you can refer them. These advisors should have a personal passion for charitable gift planning and understand your organization's mission, needs, and limitations.

NEVER STOP LEARNING

Charitable gift planning is like any other discipline. You must keep your skills sharp and your eyes and ears open to new developments. There are LOTS of resources out there to help you keep current.

Consider joining your local gift planning association. There are dozens of associations and councils around the United States. Some are large—covering a whole state or multiple states. Some are small—covering just one county or city. No matter the size, these groups are essential to your success. They bring together all kinds of people working in philanthropy and the kinds of advisors you'll want on your "bench". They offer education, networking, and support for everyone working in gift planning. I've been a member of my local association for nearly 20 years. I've volunteered as a speaker, a committee leader, and a board member. It's done wonders for my career!

Consider joining a national fundraising organization. The National Association of Charitable Gift Planners and the Association of Fundraising Professionals both offer exceptional resources to help you stay current and advance your career. Check them out.

Consider a professional designation. There are many designations you can consider. They help to further your knowledge and let others know of your particular expertise in charitable giving. Two designations I'm most familiar with are the *Certified Fund Raising Executive* (CFRE) and the *Chartered Advisor in Philanthropy* (CAP®). Both are well-recognized in this field.

Read, Read, Read......

There are so many reputable organizations that produce insightful studies on virtually every area of charitable giving. Personally, I can't wait to dive into the latest studies on things like Donor Advised Funds, Non-Cash Giving, High Net Worth Philanthropy, Qualified Charitable Distributions, and MORE! Here are just a few of the groups that regularly publish reports that I love to read as soon as they're released.

- U.S. Trust & Lily School of Philanthropy Studies on High Net Worth Philanthropy
- National Philanthropic Trust Annual Report on Donor Advised Funds
- FreeWill Reports on Qualified Charitable Distributions
- Giving USA Reports on Annual Giving in America

GATHER YOUR HELPERS

Even the largest, most sophisticated charities use helpers. No one can do it all on their own. You might need help with marketing non-cash gifts. You might need help accepting the more complex kinds of assets. You might need help with financial or legal matters. It truly does take a village. Here are some of the kinds of helpers you may want to consider to help you create the very best non-cash giving program possible.

- Your local Community Foundation
- Legal advisors
- Financial/Tax advisors
- Marketing specialists
- Professional Development providers
- Technology providers

I truly believe that YOU can be successful with non-cash gifts. With the knowledge and resources in this book, you will *Turn Wealth Into What Matters!*